LIVE
LEARN
EAT

ORO Editions
Publishers of Architecture, Art, and Design
Gordon Goff: Publisher

www.oroeditions.com
info@oroeditions.com

Published by ORO Editions

Copyright © 2020 Anthony Poon and Poon Design Inc.

All rights reserved. No part of this book may be reproduced, stored in a retrieval system, or transmitted in any form or by any means, including electronic, mechanical, photocopying of microfilming, recording, or otherwise (except that copying permitted by Sections 107 and 108 of the U.S. Copyright Law and except by reviewers for the public press) without written permission from the publisher.

You must not circulate this book in any other binding or cover and you must impose this same condition on any acquirer.

Text by Anthony Poon
Introduction by Michael Webb
Managing Editor: Jake Anderson
Book Design by Pablo Mandel / Circular Studio

Typeset in Avenir

10 9 8 7 6 5 4 3 2 1 First Edition

ISBN: 978-1-943532-72-8

Color Separations and Printing: ORO Group Ltd.
Printed in China.

ORO Editions makes a continuous effort to minimize the overall carbon footprint of its publications. As part of this goal, ORO Editions, in association with Global ReLeaf, arranges to plant trees to replace those used in the manufacturing of the paper produced for its books. Global ReLeaf is an international campaign run by American Forests, one of the world's oldest nonprofit conservation organizations. Global ReLeaf is American Forests' education and action program that helps individuals, organizations, agencies, and corporations improve the local and global environment by planting and caring for trees.

LIVE
LEARN
EAT

**ARCHITECTURE BY
ANTHONY POON**

INTRODUCTION AND EDITING BY MICHAEL WEBB

CONTENTS

7	Introduction
18	Design Your Worlds

LIVE

24	Linea: Art Gallery
40	Linea: T Plan
54	Escena: Core Wall
66	Escena: Panoramic View
74	Escena: Horizontality
80	Mixed Use: Folded Roof

LEARN

90	Greenman Elementary School
102	Feather River Academy
116	Herget Middle School
128	Bel Air Presbyterian Preschool

EAT

140	Chaya Downtown
152	Mendocino Farms
166	Din Tai Fung: The Americana At Brand
176	Din Tai Fung: South Coast Plaza
186	Vosges Haut Chocolate
200	Select Chronology 1996–2019
220	Firm Profile
221	Anthony Poon
222	Select Awards
224	Publications
225	Presentations and Image Credits
226	Acknowledgments

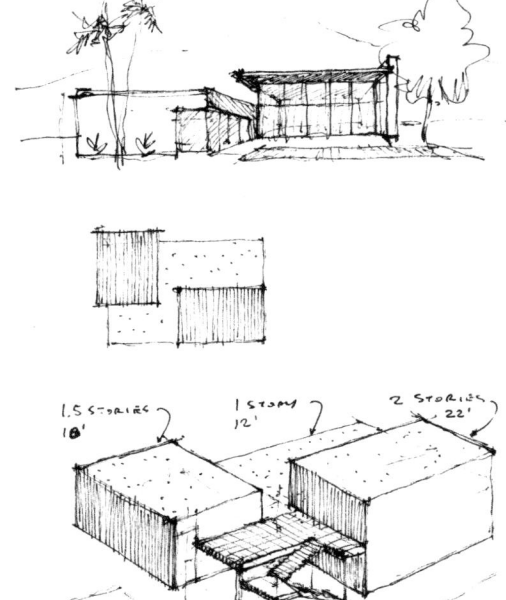
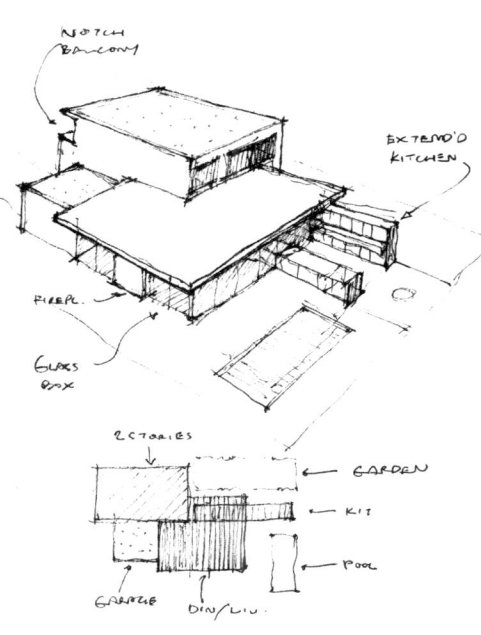
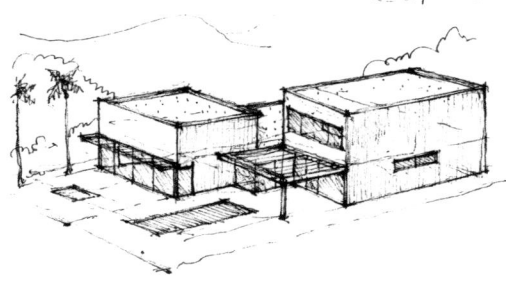

THE AGGREGATION OF
THE EXCESSIVE AGGREGATION OF SMALL
EXQUISITE THINGS INTO POWERFUL
BOLD GESTURES.

ARTISTRY, ARTISANAL
SUBLIME
GROTESQUE

DELICATE, ELEGANT, GRANDEUR IN
RAW ⇒ REFINEMENT   SMALL THINGS

PROCESS, EFFICIENCY : MACHINE
DUMPLING : METAPHOR OF CHARACTER &
                    PROCESS

CHINESE THEMES: BIG SCALE
                RE-INTERPRET'D
                ELEMENTAL MATERIALS
                ASIAN MODERN
            OF CRAFT
        VOLUME, HANDCRAFTED
    SCALE, DUMPLING, AGGREGATE
                    SMALL THINGS
                    EXQUISITE
                    SOMETHING SPECIAL

2/19/13 MAMMOTH
CUBE SCHEME

INTRODUCTION

BY MICHAEL WEBB

Anthony Poon is a pragmatic perfectionist, an architect, and artist who obsesses over the details but has a firm grasp of function and value. He has far outdistanced his peers in making good residential design more affordable by offering a range of modern tract houses that rival the best custom homes in generosity of proportion, space, and natural light at a fraction of the cost. He has designed schools that enrich the student experience and restaurants that are tailored to the needs of chefs, staff, and diners. "I revel in the scope of exploration," says Poon, "I want to design everything, to be deeply invested in all creative aspects of a project."

Add workplaces, retail, sacred spaces, cultural projects, graphics, furniture, and lighting design, and you wonder how an office of eight people can accomplish so much. The secret lies in the sharing of responsibility. Poon has assembled a multi-talented team who participate in different ways on every project. As he explains, "We always start the process with a group brainstorming session. Sometimes we play jazz for inspiration and I ask my team for ideas. If someone is passionate about a project, she takes the lead—we are flexible and non-hierarchical." For Poon, success depends in part on picking the right client—one who is open to creativity and willing to take some risks. The goal is to achieve a productive partnership and a shared vision.

Poon's own vision is holistic. Growing up in San Francisco's Chinatown, he absorbed the vitality of the local community and a city that nurtured the arts. As a child, he delighted in taking things apart and fantasizing about imaginary worlds. He secured a degree in architecture and music at the University of California, Berkeley, and wrote his master's thesis on architecture and jazz at the Harvard Graduate School of Design. He loves to draw, and most projects evolve out of sketches and physical models.

NORTH ELEVATION
1/16" = 1'-0"

Music is his passion: he began to train as a classical musician at age six, and considered making that his career. He still plays the piano every day for his own pleasure, to entertain his two daughters, and to give occasional performances. For inspiration, he listens to Beethoven—especially the late piano sonatas, which are still considered avant garde—and the dissonances of jazz pianist Thelonious Monk. "My fascination with jazz is that I can't play it," Poon explains. "I spent all those years learning the scores of Bach and Mozart and realized I'm playing someone else's notes. Whereas in jazz you come together and improvise on a theme." That seems to him a good analogy for creating architecture.

Beyond the inspiration music affords is the discipline and artistry. To excel in the classical field, one must play all the notes correctly, grasp the underlying structure of the piece and infuse the performance with feeling. Jazz is all about invention, with each musician contributing to the ensemble and then breaking out in a solo. Architecture and music have strong affinities and they give Poon's work its harmony, rhythm, and resonance.

This monograph explores three fields in which Poon Design has excelled; housing, schools, and restaurants. Each is linked to the others. Living, learning, and eating are universal human activities, and they all involve social interaction. A house is at once shelter—a place to eat, sleep, and entertain—and a nest in which to nurture a family or to work in a home office. The architecture of a school shapes lives, facilitates teaching, and promotes friendships that may last a lifetime. After hours, it may serve as a community center or a resource for evening classes. In a restaurant, circulation is the key to smooth operation and efficient service, and the layout of the kitchen is even more important than the arrangement of seating. Once the logistical issues have been resolved, architects strive to create a compelling ambience. From fast food to fine dining, a restaurant may have to accommodate a hurried lunch, romantic tryst, or boisterous reception. Poon Design explores all these options in their designs, so that each of their buildings plays multiple roles.

They've designed custom homes for affluent clients and have spent the past 16 years enhancing and extending a 1920s Gordon Kaufmann estate in Beverly Hills for a tycoon who has many other homes. It takes skill, diplomacy, and persistence to see such projects through to completion. Poon is well versed in that quarter but prefers to follow the lead of the pioneering Modernists bringing good design to a wider public. In 2010 he seized an opportunity to put that philosophy into practice. An enlightened Texas developer-designer, Andrew Adler of the Alta Verde Group, invited Poon Design to build high-quality modern houses for less than $150 a square foot—a fraction of their budget for one-offs. The developer acquired four tracts of land in and around Palm Springs at a bargain price following the recession and wanted to create model communities.

Poon responded to the challenge, designing four models of different sizes and configurations over the 18 months Adler was raising funds for the development. Years later, Poon added 16 more house models. To cut costs and speed construction, the architects stripped their models of everything that could be considered inessential, simplifying the floor plans and developing new concepts for walls and roof. Many architects have experimented with prefabrication to rationalize home building just as cars are mass produced on a production line and sold with minor variations. But people demand more from their homes, driven by fantasies and a desire for uniqueness, even in the suburbs. Poon has found the middle ground between custom and production housing.

At the developer's first community, Alta Verde Escena, the base model has a spinal wall containing all the building services, dividing an open-plan living area from the sleeping zone. The roof is a factory-made assembly, comprising trusses made with the bottom chord as the finished ceiling joists, eliminating the need to frame a ceiling. Parapet and rooftop framing with slopes and crickets for drainage also come prefabricated with the roof assembly, saving on additional labor and materials. Typically, ducts are located atop the roof and have to be wrapped; here they are embedded in insulation that was blown in from the bottom through netting suspended from the top chord.

Outer walls have expansive double glazing and are shaded from the desert sun by a projecting roof plane. The materials are basic—precast concrete, painted stucco, drywall, and porcelain tile floors, since wood floors cannot survive desert heat and sand. Hollow core fiberglass doors are filled with lightweight concrete giving the doors a luxurious feel, and providing security and an acoustic barrier at low cost. The general contractor was well coached and trained the subs to achieve a high standard of finish and detailing. The contractor offered a good price for the first 12 roof assemblies in anticipation of the 200 that would follow.

House sizes range from 2,300 to 4,800 square feet, and the larger models—called Linea—employ the same materials as Escena, but offer higher ceilings and greater expanses of glazing to pull in natural light. To avert monotony, eight different designs alternate in the first development of 130 homes, and a similar variety is evident in the other three developments. A total of 225 houses have been built and sold, and they form pleasing

ensembles. Poon demonstrates that you can create a community of modern houses that are subtly varied, just as Gregory Ain did in the Mar Vista tract of Los Angeles, 70 years ago. There, about 50 identical houses are rotated to create a rhythmic variation from one to the next. Poon varies the façade treatment of the white Linea houses, adding grilles and columns to catch the sunlight and cast shadows across expanses of white stucco. In the larger Escena estate, materials and desert tones are varied from one house to the next.

This project explodes two myths: that an architect-designed house has to be more expensive than an off-the-shelf builder's model; and second, that the market for tract homes won't embrace innovation. Poon's designs are uncompromising: clean lines, unadorned surfaces, expansive glass sliders opening onto the back yards, with nowhere to hide clutter, but they've sold at a faster rate than other local tracts—evidence of how modernism has become widely accepted in Palm Springs. And—though Poon values spontaneity in the creative process—he insists that the owners of his houses should not make changes or additions. "They sign a covenant and the city enforces it," he explains. "We've tailored these houses carefully, and we don't want them messed up."

Before establishing his own practice in 2001, Poon worked for other firms. At the hydra-headed NBBJ he worked on large-scale sports projects and was put in charge of a 380,000 square-foot convocation center for Xavier University in Cincinnati. Persuading a conservative Jesuit school that a modern precast concrete block was an appropriate addition to a Gothic-revival campus boosted the confidence of a tyro architect. Further encouragement came during his stay at Hardy Holzman Pfeiffer Associates, where he collaborated on the design of performing arts centers, civic buildings, and museums.

That experience led him to take on another ambitious project after going independent. Poon co-founded Architecture for Education with partner Gaylaird Christopher and, in 2002, the 12-person firm was commissioned to master-plan the West Aurora School District, in Illinois. Soon after, they were invited to renovate or extend 16 schools in the district, and to team with a local firm to create two new campuses, following months of research and discussions with the teachers. Later, Architecture for Education would team with two larger firms to design two new high schools in Los Angeles. Though each project was applauded by its users, the opportunity to build on this experience has become more challenging. Today, the requests for proposals sent out by public educational authorities ask architects to list five schools they have built in the last five years, privileging larger firms. The assumption that size connotes quality ensures that the same large firms are hired to design hospitals and sports stadia, stifling innovation and shutting out small practices. Privately funded institutions are more willing to judge proposals on their merits, and Poon is currently working on additions to a K-8 school in Los Angeles.

No such restrictions apply to the design of restaurants and Poon Design have more than 40 to their credit, ranging from unpretentious snack bars to the luxurious Chaya in downtown Los Angeles. There, the Japanese client was unconcerned about cost, but most restaurants have a tight budget and need to be delivered in a few months. Yet each is a unique challenge and involves a multitude of competing demands. The kitchen has to be configured for smooth operation by as few staff as possible—

this is the biggest cost—and have the capacity to serve all the tables promptly. It is also shaped by the type of food served and the philosophy of the chef. There has to be a smooth interplay between staff and diners, and their movements have to be plotted in advance—much like a coach marking up a whiteboard for a football team.

Success depends on the customer experience—of food, service, and atmosphere—and most restaurants fail the test and are out of business in a year. Poon sees his team as choreographers, ensuring that every move will be graceful, free-flowing, and timely. They understand that lighting and music tracks have to be calibrated, changing through the day from brunch, to happy hour, dinner, and late-night drinks. And they like to design every element from signage to menus and staff uniforms.

A major commission came from Din Tai Fung, a Taiwanese restaurant chain that made a humble US debut in an East LA storefront and now has 150 branches worldwide. Their Chinese dumplings have won raves and people are willing to wait hours for a table. After dining at Chaya, the owner of Din Tai Fung commissioned Poon to design two flagship restaurants in prestigious southern California locations. One was in Glendale, the other in the South Coast Plaza shopping center, where the new structure replaced a McDonald's and became a destination that boosted business for the nearby stores. The architects extended the footprint to include a dining terrace and a take-out counter and used laser-cut screens to shield the façade and create intimate dining areas. The centerpiece is a glass-walled kitchen as clean as a lab in which chefs prepare the hand-made dumplings in a riveting display of virtuosity.

"As a musician and artist, I'd like to continue our pursuit of arts buildings, and work on a larger scale," says Poon. "All the projects we've done contain the seeds of larger buildings, including museums, libraries, theaters, civic, and performing arts centers." He demonstrated his ability to handle ambitious jobs at the start of his career and everything he has done over the past two decades has prepared him for greater challenges. He has a strong commitment to sustainability, in his work and within his office, and a desire to incorporate green public spaces into every kind of building. He has no illusions that the leap will be easy. "It's the path of an architect: one project leads to another," he admits. "Hard work—I don't believe in the lottery ticket."

Michael Webb has authored 25 books on architecture and design, most recently *Architects' Houses,* and a memoir, *Moving Around: A Lifetime of Wandering,* while editing and contributing essays to a score of monographs. He is also a regular contributor to leading journals in the United States, Asia, and Europe.

DESIGN YOUR WORLDS

BY ANTHONY POON

There are so many monographs with so many beautiful photos of architecture; so many coffee table books of extraordinary designs, heroic forms, and exquisite details.

When approached to create this monograph, I hesitated. I did not want to create yet another catalog of glossy pictures. After all, the images and descriptions of our work at Poon Design Inc. are already out there for public consumption, in print and digitally. If I were to offer a monograph to a broad audience of readers and design enthusiasts, I wanted this book to tell a story. Through an illustrated volume on our architecture, I wanted to take a position, display the creative journey, and to hopefully prove a thesis or two.

We titled the book *Live Learn Eat* because whether a house, school, or restaurant, we believe that architecture enables life to be vibrant—to resonate. The best designs do not need to break the bank. We pride ourselves on the creativity that captures the ambitions and stories of our clients with value in the foreground.

Yes, we strive to make our architecture handsome and striking, but our work communicates more than aesthetics. Our designs communicate ideas, expressing everything from our culture and the community we live in, to the specific needs and solutions for each client. We call this content; each and every client of ours has ambitions for their existence, memories of past successes, and lessons learned. These ideas, dreams, and stories are the basis for our design process.

Regarding the artistic journey, I enjoy looking at how ideas are conceived. In any architect's monograph, I seek more than the attractive photography of a completed building, but rather, how did the architect get there? What are the hundred steps, missteps, and side steps—from the very first sketch on the back of a napkin to the finished project? A monograph should dedicate some of the graphic real estate of the pages to the journey, showing us the roses that are noticed along the path, as well as the thorns. Hopefully, *Live Learn Eat* provides a glimpse into how things take shape.

Some would call me a busy-body. I have many interests, hobbies, and fields of pursuit. I paint, collage, and sculpt. I play piano and once in a while compose music. I write essays and publish here and there. I even scrapbook, tie dye, and make furniture. Amongst such artsy explorations, I add the ingredient of architecture.

For a recent podcast, the interviewer asked me, "Of your various activities, what creative pursuit do you like best?" Akin to the challenges of identifying one's favorite rock band or flavor of ice cream, there is no reasonable answer. Do I like playing a Beethoven piano sonata more than writing a position article on the design industry? Do I enjoy working on a large mixed-media art piece more than designing a Buddhist temple? I don't see any such exercises as separate, or, in any way, independent from each other. Artistic endeavors are not discrete. All my investigations, experiments, tests, and failures fall under the shelter of a single umbrella, a simultaneous effort—that of a creative voyage with no starting point, and, excitingly, no end in sight.

When one plant species pollinates another, the cross pollination creates new varieties of plant life. So too should all forms of artistic study and all mediums of imagination and expression. Why can't the performance of Brahms cross pollinate with how we design a library? Why can't a poem be the catalyst for a painting? Or music, painting, writing, architecture, and so on? For me, it is all one artistic gesture—interconnected, intertwined, and inseparable.

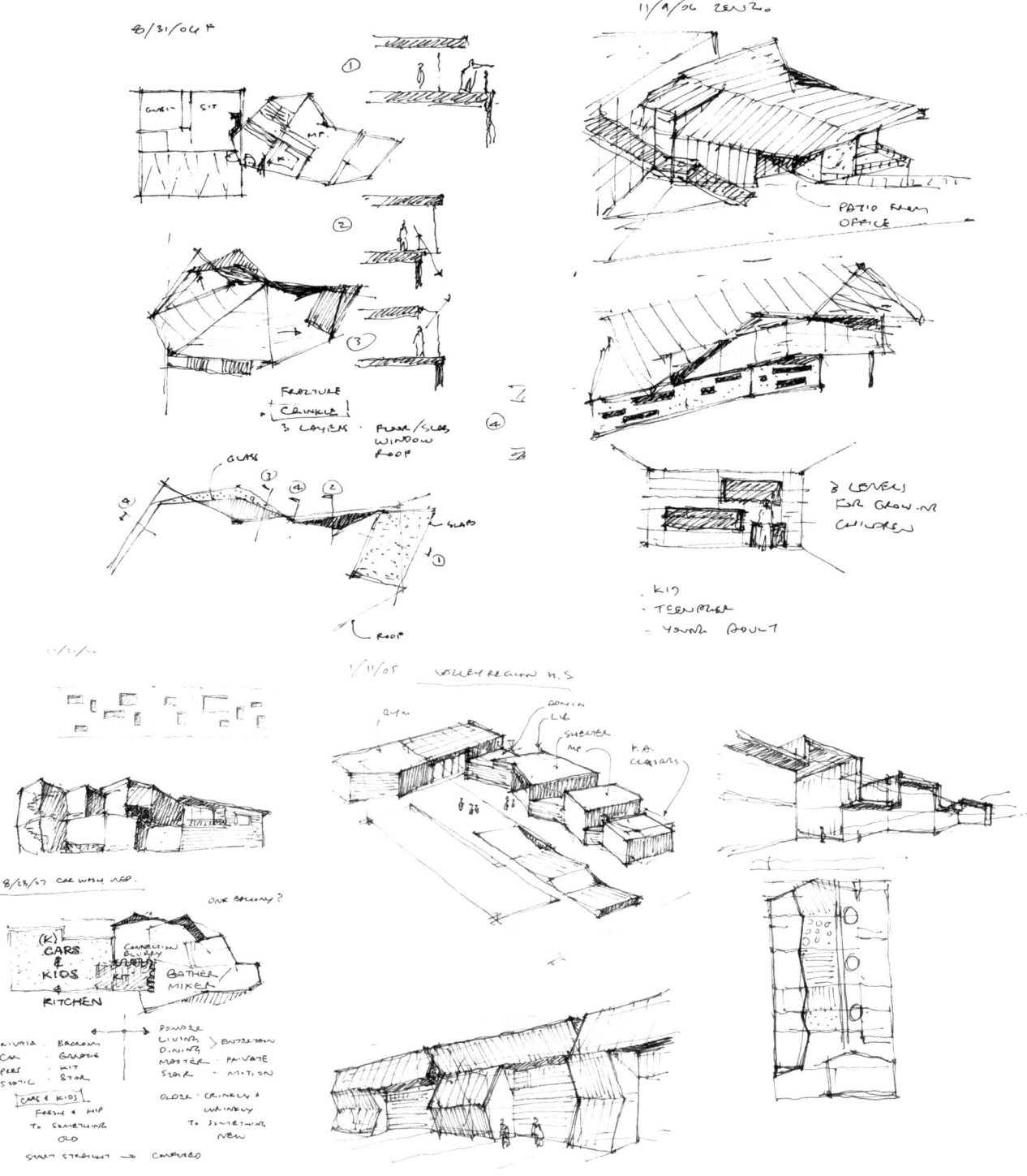

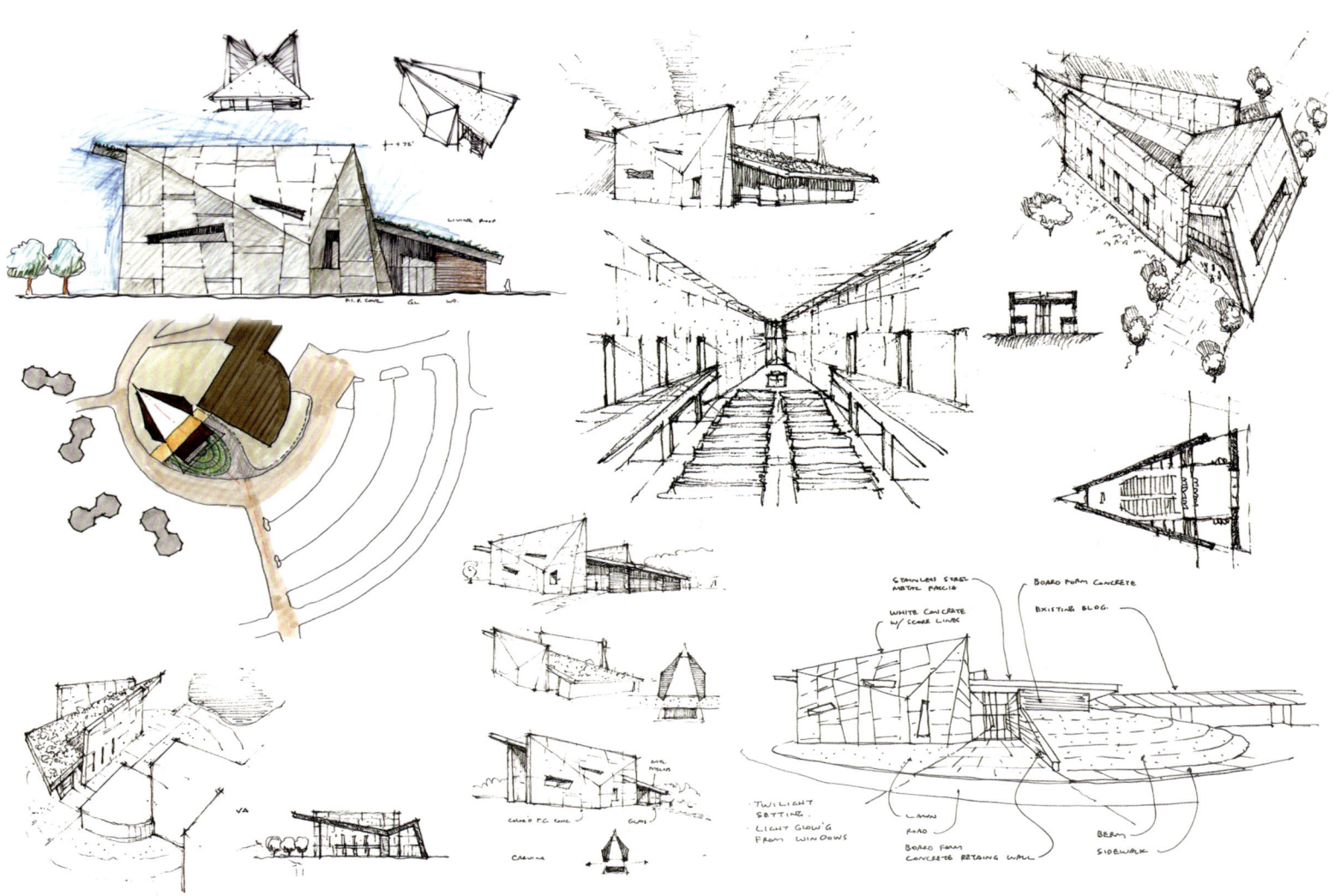

ADLER HOMES

ADLER / POON DESIGN PARTNERSHIP

The following five works in this section, entitled "Live," are the results of a collaboration between Andrew Adler and Anthony Poon. Mr. Adler is a designer and developer of residential communities of architectural merit, and his works are widely heralded, having graced the pages of numerous publications, as well as receiving national accolades spanning 25 years (select housing awards listed on page 222).

The projects exhibited here demonstrate Adler's ideas: Infuse American housing with only the essentials of worthy design features, such as natural light and a central element of architectural drama. The following home called Escena: Core Wall employs a continuous central utility wall—a powerful linear element contrasted with expansive walls of glass and measured proportions. No matter the size and scale, from large estates at the Linea projects to the efficient 2,400-square-foot-compositions at Escena, Adler's execution of the idiom "less is more" resonates.

In 2008, Adler commissioned Anthony Poon and his architecture studio, Poon Design Inc. With artistry and technical savvy in the design process, the Adler / Poon partnership delivered four exciting housing communities under Adler's real estate development company, Alta Verde Group. Over seven years, the hands-on creative journey brought together two minds with differing but complementary design skills. The collaboration delivered over 200 homes and won over 20 national design and housing awards—boasting one of highest honors in North America: the 2018 Best in Housing, from the American Institute of Architects. Constructed at a fraction of the cost of custom homes, the Adler / Poon partnership for these projects have ignited an entirely new movement of housing design and demographics in the region, extending beyond the boundaries of Southern California.

ADLER HOMES

ADLER / POON DESIGN PARTNERSHIP

In 2008, Adler commissioned Anthony Poon and his architecture studio, Poon Design Inc. With artistry and technical savvy in the design process, the Adler / Poon partnership delivered four exciting housing communities under Adler's real estate development company, Alta Verde Group. Over seven years, the hands-on creative journey brought together two minds with differing but complementary design skills. The collaboration delivered over 200 homes and won over 20 national design and housing awards—boasting one of highest honors in North America: the 2018 Best in Housing, from the American Institute of Architects. Constructed at a fraction of the cost of custom homes, the Adler / Poon partnership for these projects have ignited an entirely new movement of housing design and demographics in the region, extending beyond the boundaries of Southern California.

The following five works in this section, entitled "Live," are the results of a collaboration between Andrew Adler and Anthony Poon. Mr. Adler is a designer and developer of residential communities of architectural merit, and his works are widely heralded, having graced the pages of numerous publications, as well as receiving national accolades spanning 25 years (select housing awards listed on page 222).

The projects exhibited here demonstrate Adler's ideas: infuse American housing with only the essentials of worthy design features, such as natural light and a central element of architectural drama. The following home called Escena: Core Wall employs a continuous central utility wall—a powerful linear element contrasted with expansive walls of glass and measured proportions. No matter the size and scale, from large estates at the Linea projects to the efficient 2,400-square-foot-compositions at Escena, Adler's execution of the idiom "less is more," resonates.

LIVE

LINEA: ART GALLERY

PALM SPRINGS, CALIFORNIA

Crisp lines, expansive glazing, measured proportions, and sculptural massing characterize a house that is spacious and affordable. A hundred feet of 11-foot-tall glass sliding doors infuse the 4,790-square-foot, four-bedroom tract house with natural light, capture views of the mountains, and encourage indoor-outdoor living on all but the hottest days. Features include steel grid screens, a colonnade of steel pipe columns, and 6kw rooftop solar panels. The combination of transparency and opacity was inspired by such minimalist artists as Donald Judd and Robert Morris. (Associate architect: Prest Vuksic Architects.)

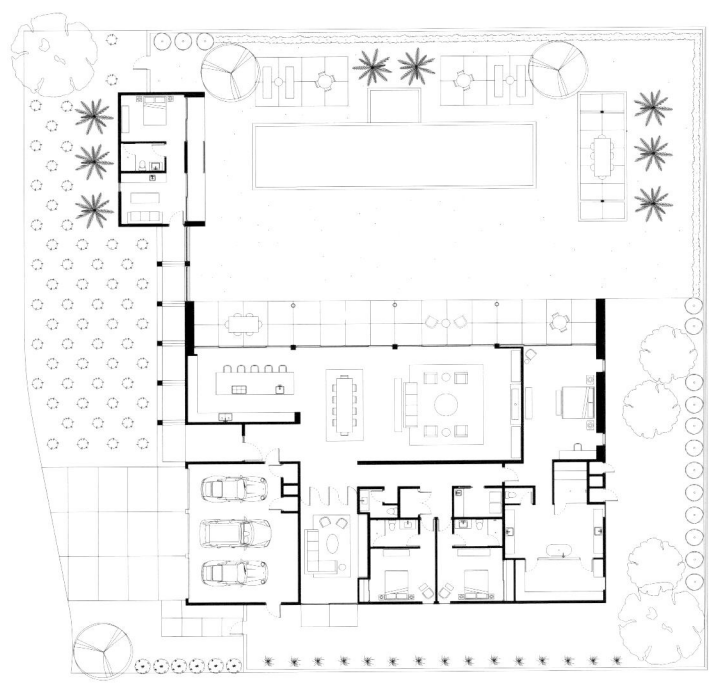

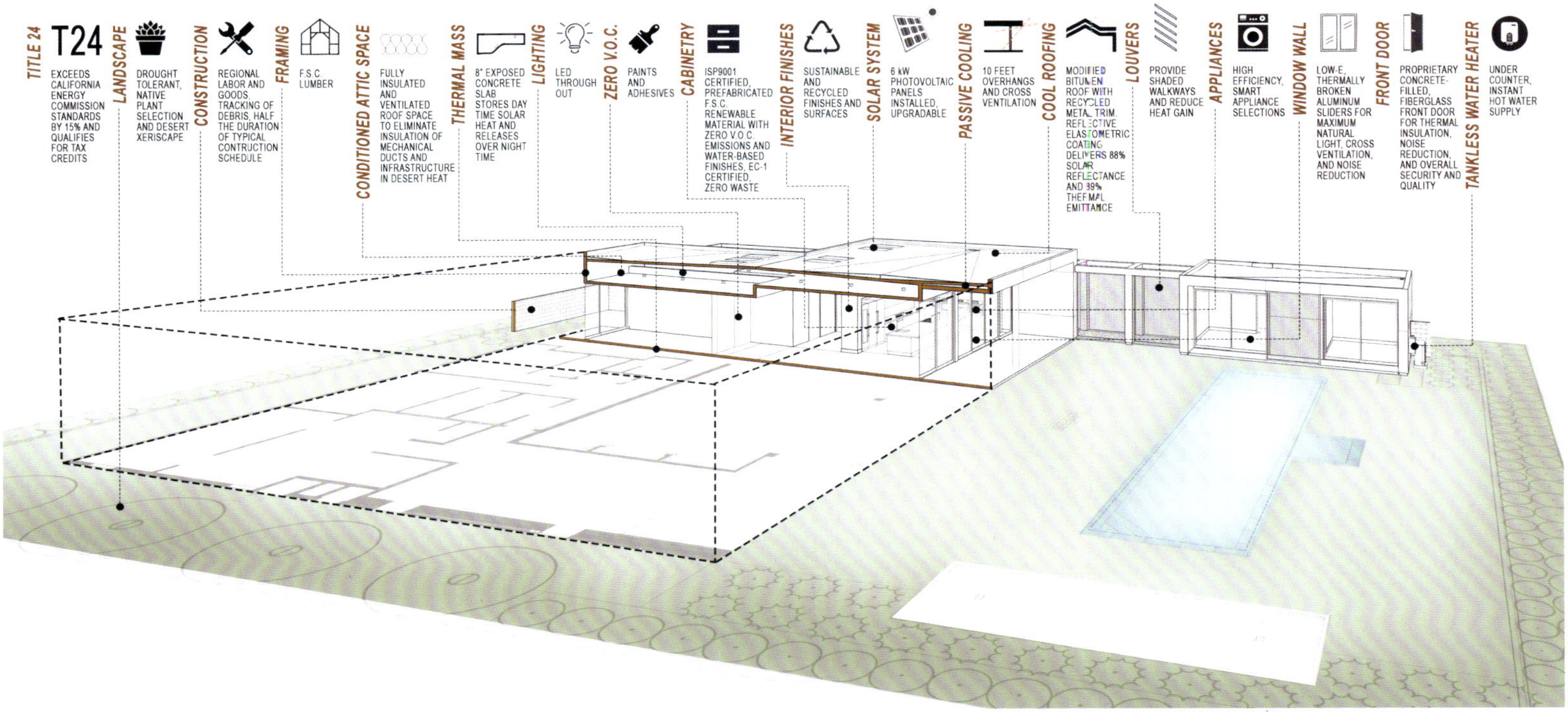

TITLE 24	**T24**	EXCEEDS CALIFORNIA ENERGY COMMISSION STANDARDS BY 15% AND QUALIFIES FOR TAX CREDITS
LANDSCAPE		DROUGHT TOLERANT, NATIVE PLANT SELECTION, AND DESERT XERISCAPE
CONSTRUCTION		REGIONAL LABOR AND GOODS, TRACKING OF DEBRIS, HALF THE DURATION OF TYPICAL CONTRUCTION SCHEDULE
FRAMING		F.S.C. LUMBER
CONDITIONED ATTIC SPACE		FULLY INSULATED AND VENTILATED ROOF SPACE TO ELIMINATE INSULATION OF MECHANICAL DUCTS AND INFRASTRUCTURE IN DESERT HEAT
THERMAL MASS		8" EXPOSED CONCRETE SLAB STORES DAY TIME SOLAR HEAT AND RELEASES OVER NIGHT TIME
LIGHTING		LED THROUGH OUT
ZERO V.O.C.		PAINTS AND ADHESIVES
CABINETRY		ISP9001 CERTIFIED, PREFABRICATED F.S.C. RENEWABLE MATERIAL WITH ZERO V.O.C. EMISSIONS AND WATER-BASED FINISHES, EC-1 CERTIFIED, ZERO WASTE
INTERIOR FINISHES		SUSTAINABLE AND RECYCLED FINISHES AND SURFACES
SOLAR SYSTEM		6 kW PHOTOVOLTAIC PANELS INSTALLED, UPGRADABLE
PASSIVE COOLING		10 FEET OVERHANGS AND CROSS VENTILATION
COOL ROOFING		MODIFIED BITUMEN ROOF WITH RECYCLED METAL TRIM. REFLECTIVE ELASTOMETRIC COATING DELIVERS 88% SOLAR REFLECTANCE AND 99% THERMAL EMITTANCE
LOUVERS		PROVIDE SHADED WALKWAYS AND REDUCE HEAT GAIN
APPLIANCES		HIGH EFFICIENCY, SMART APPLIANCE SELECTIONS
WINDOW WALL		LOW-E THERMALLY BROKEN ALUMINUM SLIDERS FOR MAXIMUM NATURAL LIGHT, CROSS VENTILATION, AND NOISE REDUCTION
FRONT DOOR		PROPRIETARY CONCRETE-FILLED, FIBERGLASS FRONT DOOR FOR THERMAL INSULATION, NOISE REDUCTION, AND OVERALL SECURITY AND QUALITY
TANKLESS WATER HEATER		UNDER COUNTER, INSTANT HOT WATER SUPPLY

LINEA: T PLAN

PALM SPRINGS, CALIFORNIA

Behind the street façade of large, white plaster panels with louvered slots is a glass box. The open living room, dining room, and kitchen have wall-to-wall, floor-to-ceiling glass walls on opposite sides. This great room offers a 22-foot-long kitchen island and indoor/outdoor living under the deep roof overhangs. The 4,870-square-foot, four-bedroom tract home is stripped of unnecessary ornament. The white architecture and white furniture offer a blank canvas for the inhabitants to add the colors of their existence. (Associate architect: Prest Vuksic Architects.)

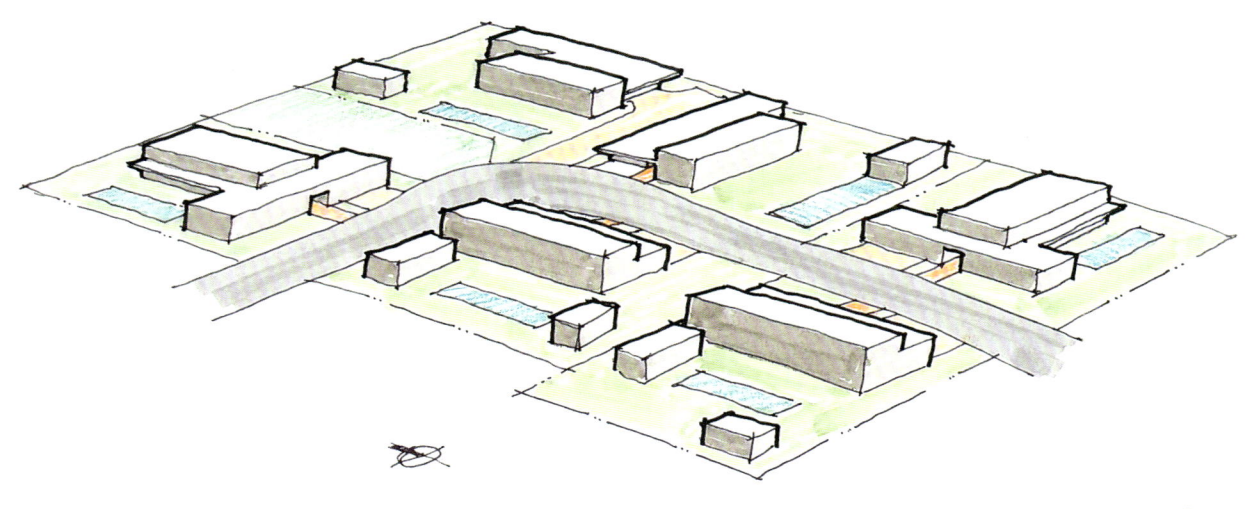

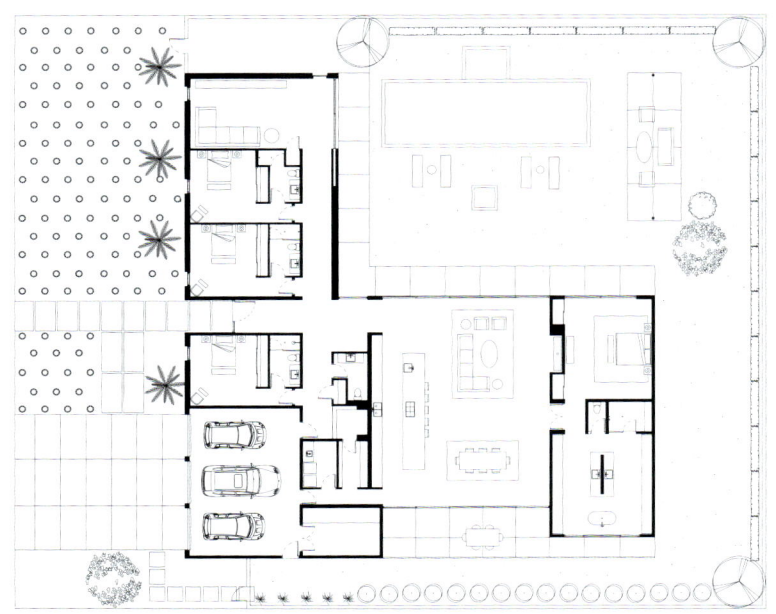

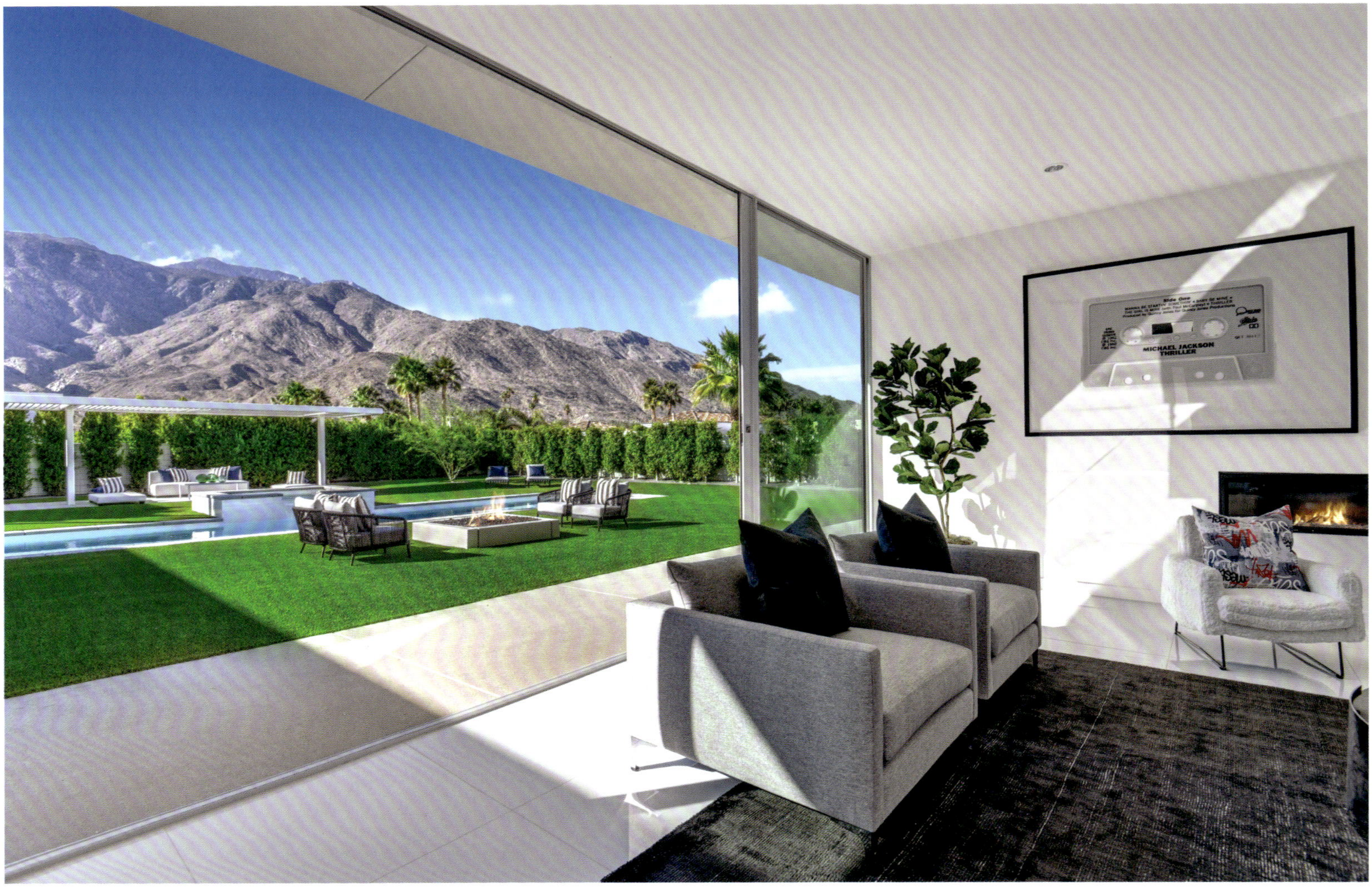
Side One
MICHAEL JACKSON
THRILLER

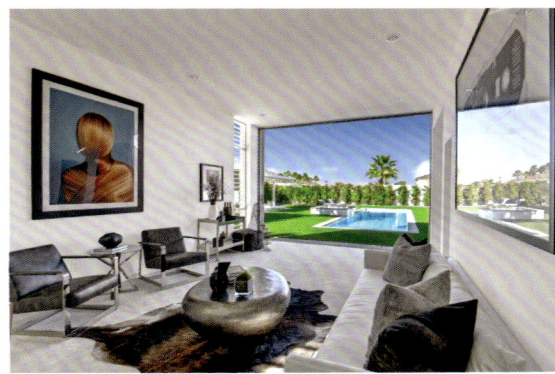

ESCENA: CORE WALL

PALM SPRINGS, CALIFORNIA

Adjacent to a public golf course, this compact prototype sits on a property only 55 feet wide. The 2,610-square-foot, three-bedroom residence is split down the middle by a continuous white wall. One half comprises the public functions in an open floor plan: entry, kitchen, dining room, and living room. The other half contains the private functions such as bedrooms, bathrooms, and a home office. The thick, white dividing wall runs 100 feet from end to end of the home, and contains the mechanical and plumbing systems, smart technology, security, AV, storage, etc. Features include Italian cabinets with commercial appliances, and a 2kW rooftop solar array on a reflective, energy-efficient roof. The master bathroom has separate dressing areas that connect at a wet zone with a free-standing soaking tub.

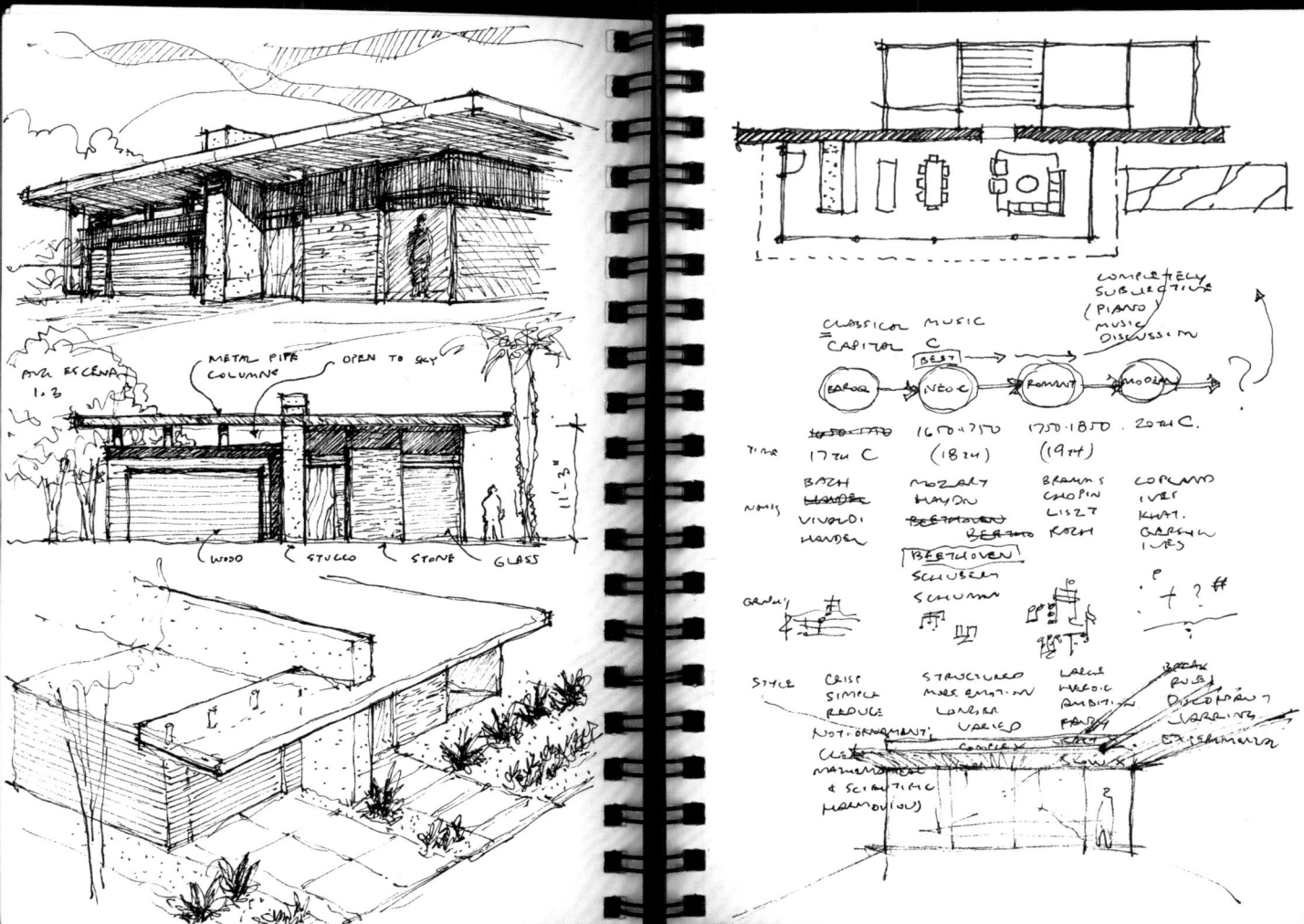

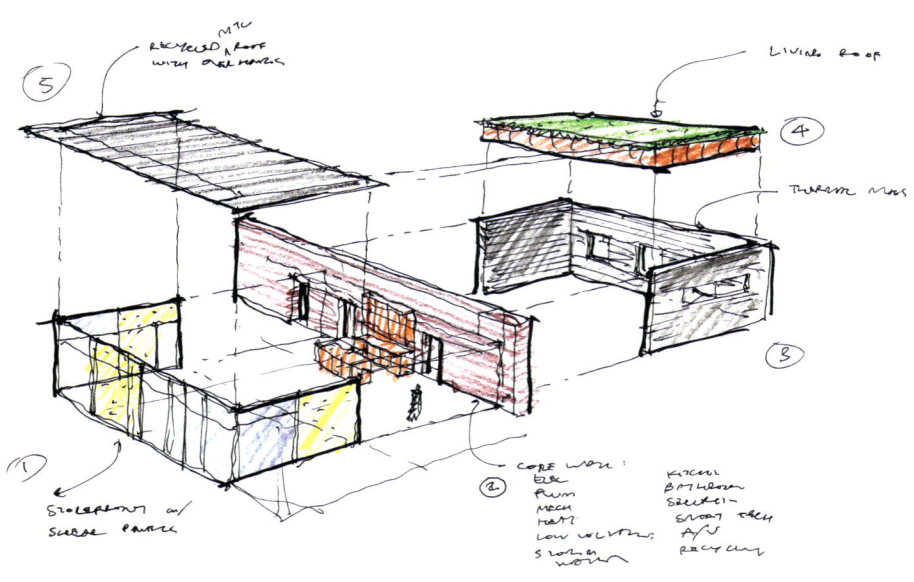

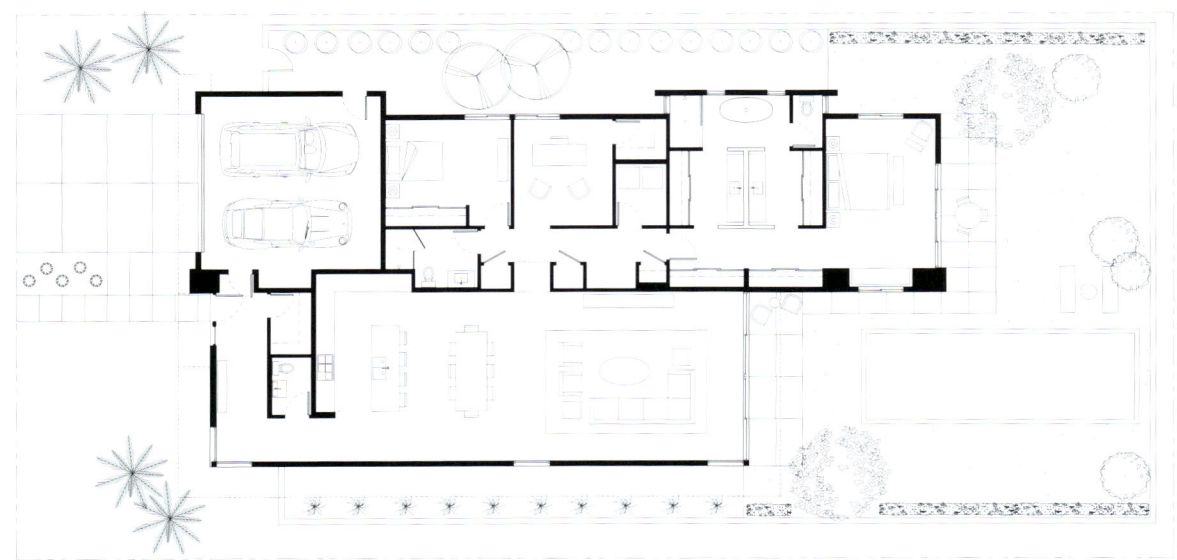

65

ESCENA: PANORAMIC VIEW

PALM SPRINGS, CALIFORNIA

The "P" in the name stands for the panoramic views of the golf course, through the living room's 36-foot wide, 11-foot-tall, wall-to-wall, glass sliding doors. Along with a private patio, the master bedroom also shares this view. The abundance of natural light at the rear of this 2,560-square-foot, three-bedroom residence contrasts with the windowless street façade accented by a compositional white frame. The wide central hallway serves as both an art gallery and the spine that draws a visitor from the front door to the views at the rear of property.

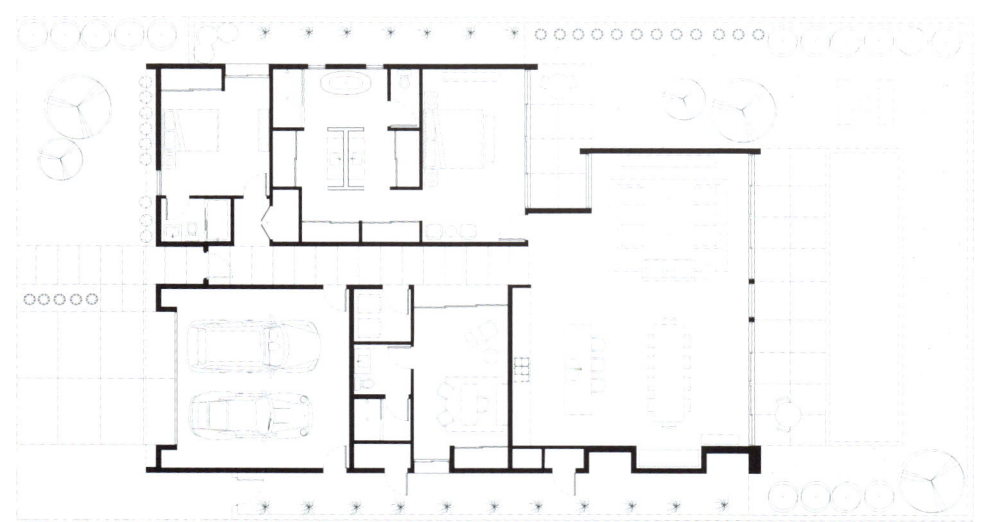

ESCENA: HORIZONTALITY

PALM SPRINGS, CALIFORNIA

This model is designed for properties where only the front of the site has mountain views. The 2,650-square-foot, three-bedroom production house is situated at the rear of the property allowing for a large gated front yard with swimming pool, which takes best advantage of sun and views. Alongside the open and flexible living room, dining room, and kitchen, the main circulation extends from the front of the property through the house, to a small sculpture garden at the rear. A palm tree at the entry pokes through an opening in the roof overhang, referencing a feature of Palm Springs Modernism.

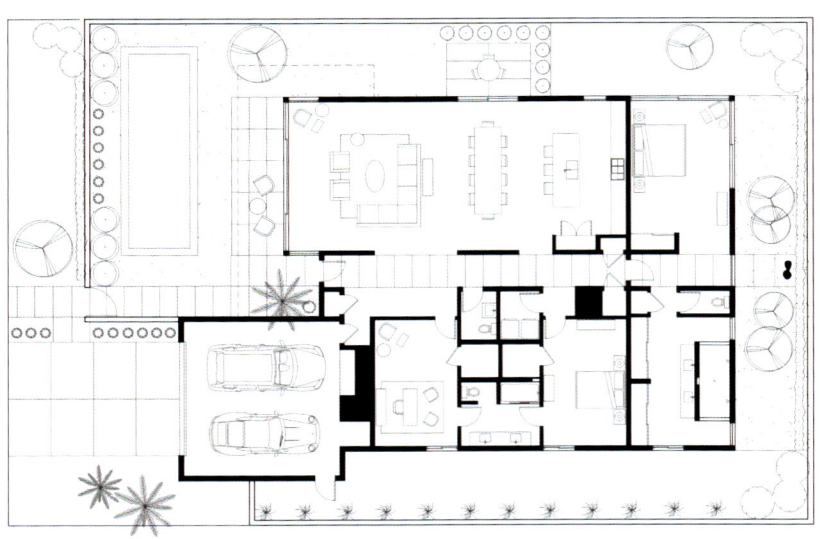

MIXED-USE: FOLDED ROOF

MANHATTAN BEACH, CALIFORNIA

This is a 13,600-square-foot, mixed-use project located on a compact urban site with a dozen underground parking spaces. The site is sliced into four segments: one commercial and three residential. Street level office space comprises 1,100 square feet. The three two-story residences vary between 1,500 and 2,000 square feet, and have a green roof overlooking the ocean. Between the roof folds, natural light filters into the residential units. The residences on the second floor are "pushed and pulled" so as to reduce the scale of the building. The first residence is slid to the front, giving it a back patio in addition to the large side yard. The second residence is slid to the back to have a front patio. And the third residence is slid halfway, with a patio in front and back. (With Lazar Design/Build.)

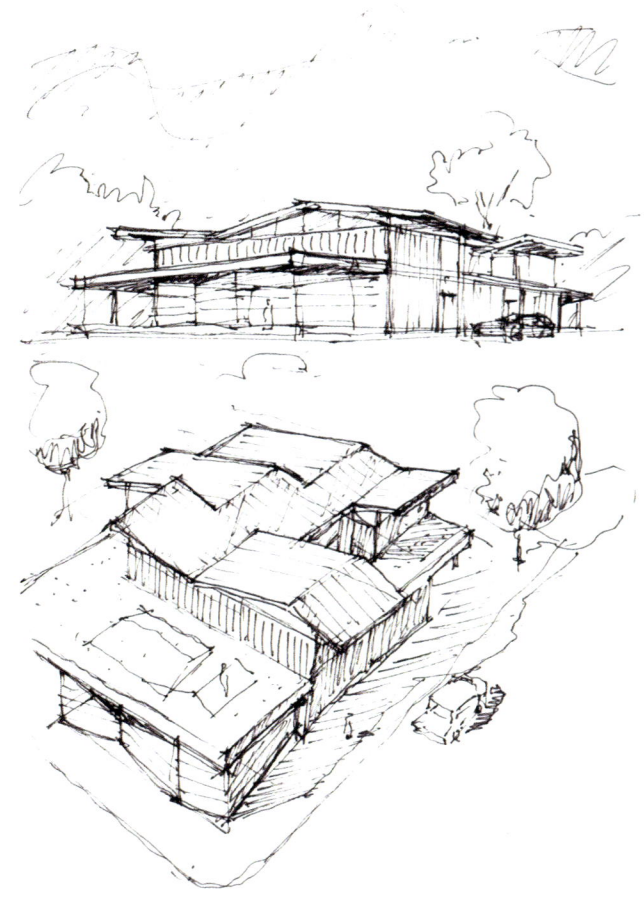

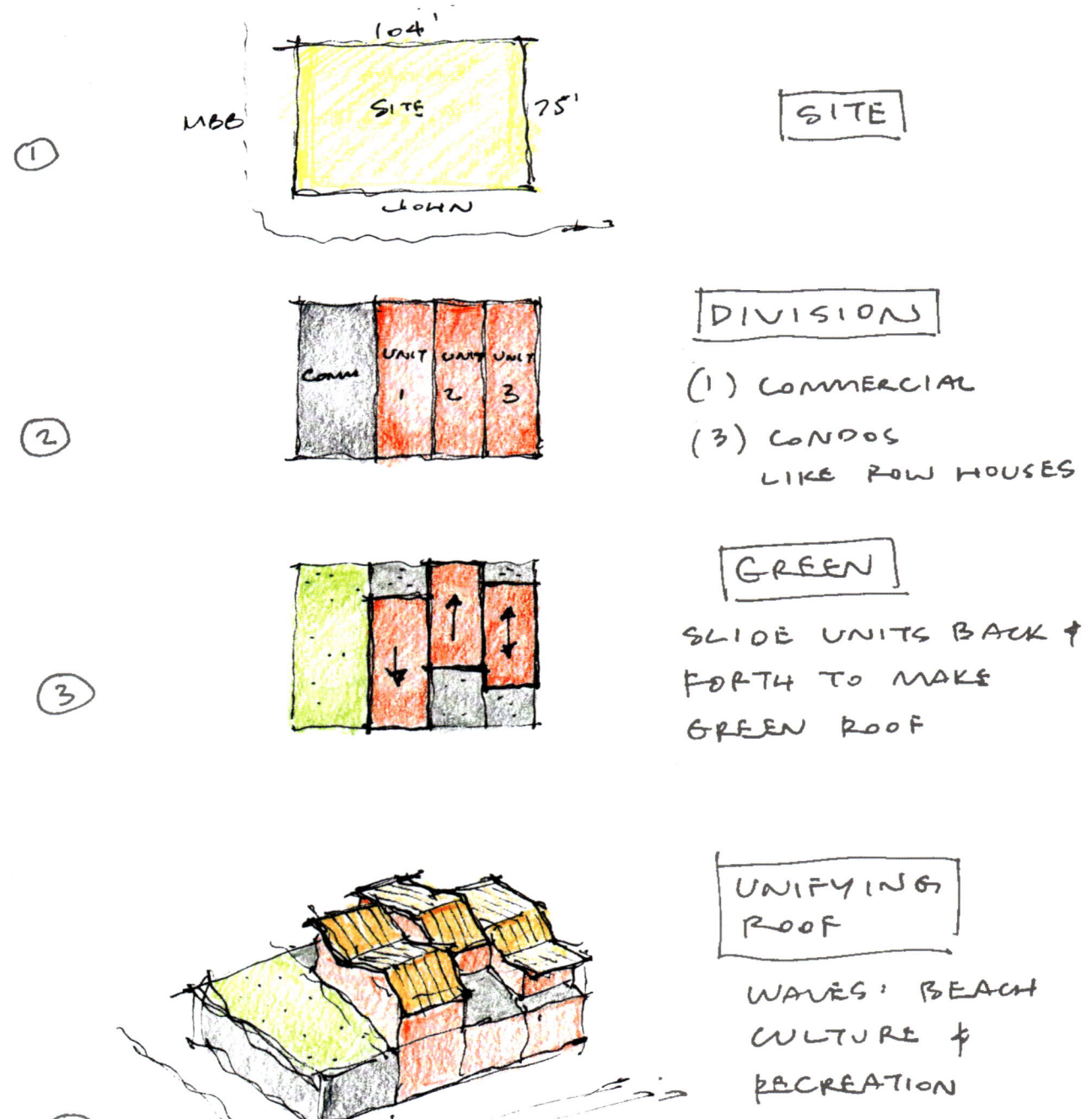

① SITE

② DIVISION
(1) COMMERCIAL
(3) CONDOS LIKE ROW HOUSES

③ GREEN
SLIDE UNITS BACK & FORTH TO MAKE GREEN ROOF

④ UNIFYING ROOF
WAVES: BEACH CULTURE & RECREATION

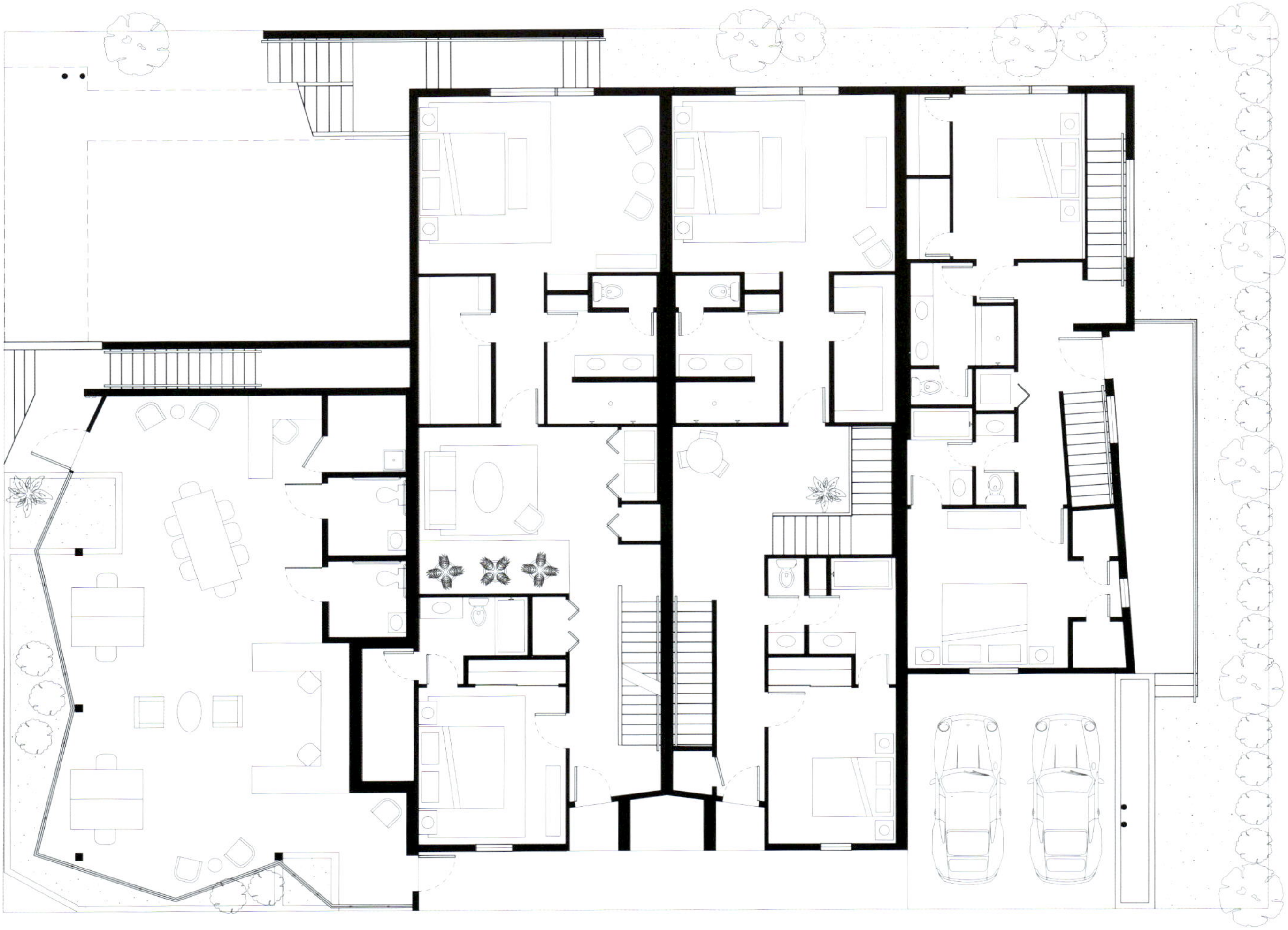

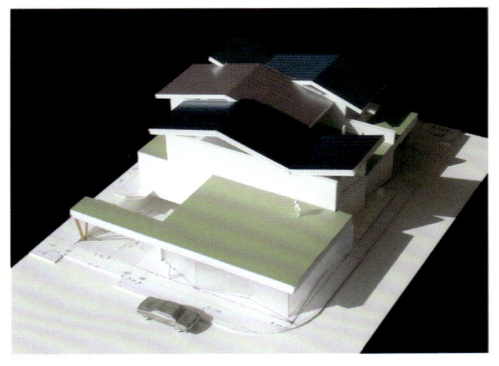
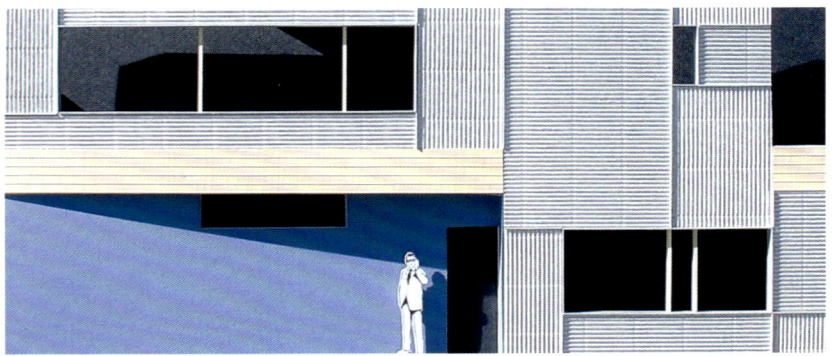

LEARN

GREENMAN ELEMENTARY SCHOOL

AURORA, ILLINOIS

This new 62,500-square-foot school is designed to foster the performing arts. The stage of the multipurpose room is double sided, providing a formal stage for performances to the multipurpose auditorium, and an informal stage to the school's lobby. The extra-wide stair leading to the second floor doubles as amphitheater seating. Second-story balconies overlook double height spaces. On the outside, various window compositions express rhythm and harmony. The 700 students are assigned to seven learning communities. In partnership with Aurora University, this elementary school has facilities for hands-on, in-classroom training of future teachers. YMCA's preschool program provides preschool facilities adjacent to the kindergarten classroom. (Architecture for Education, with associate architect, Cordogan, Clark & Associates.)

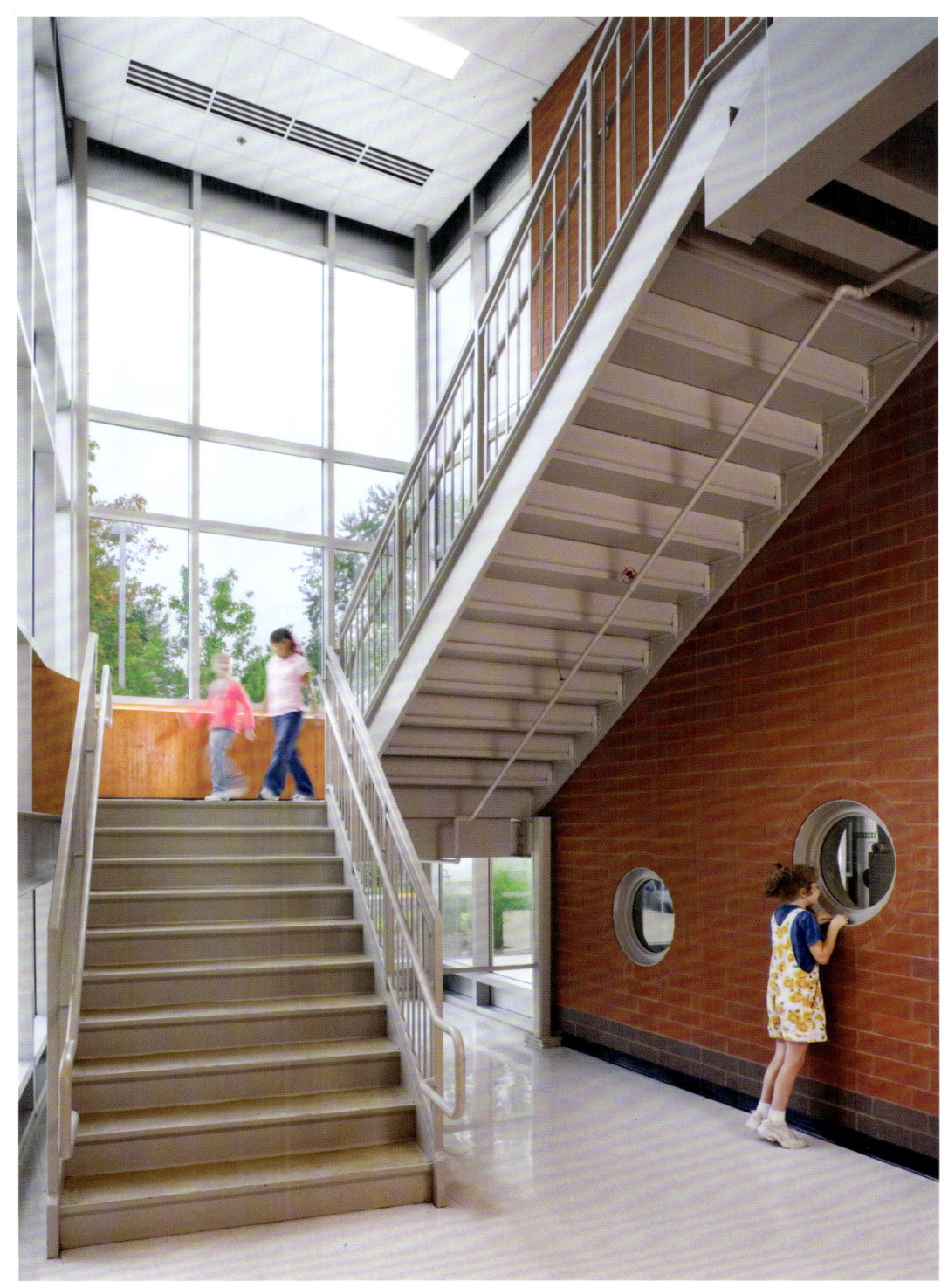

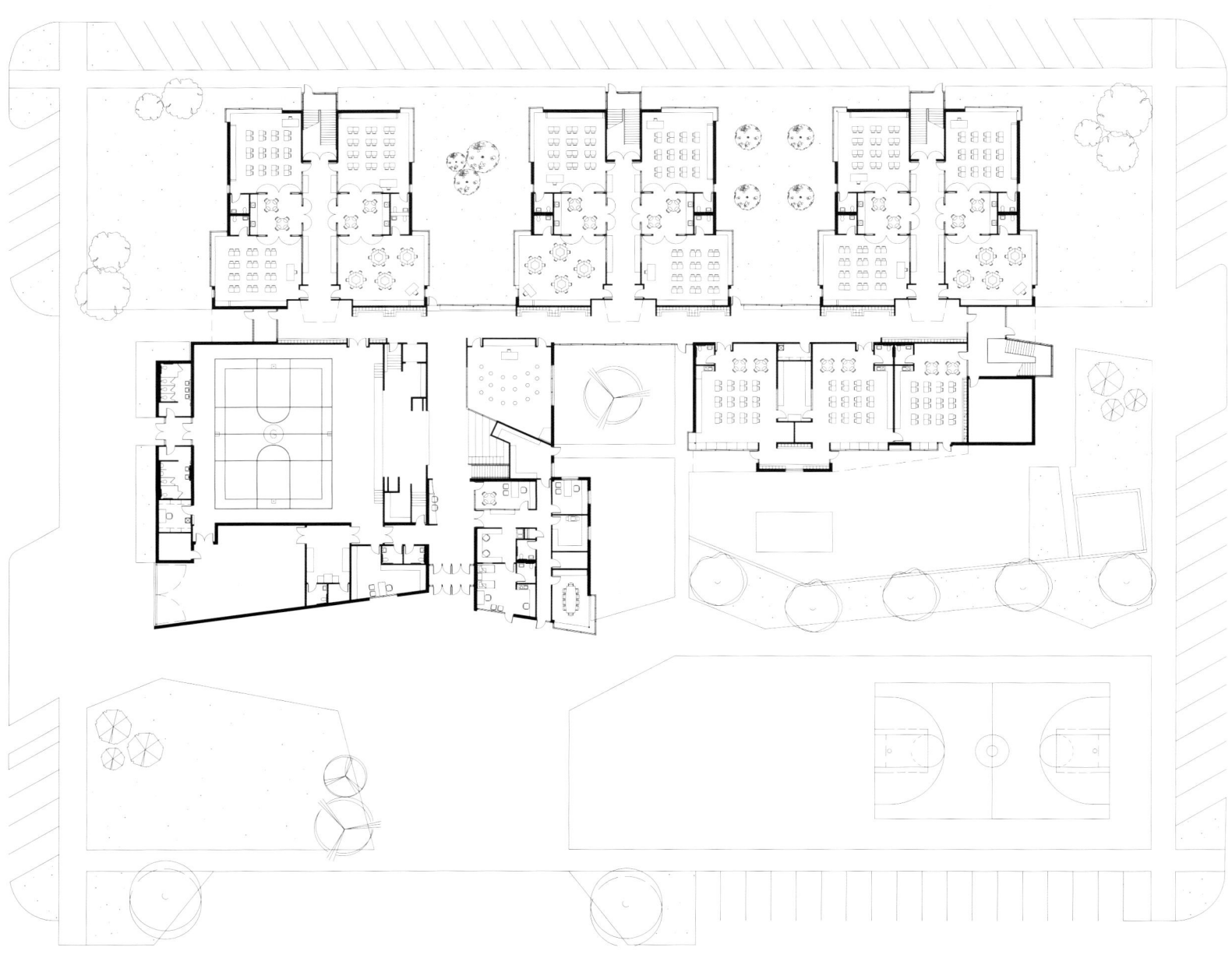

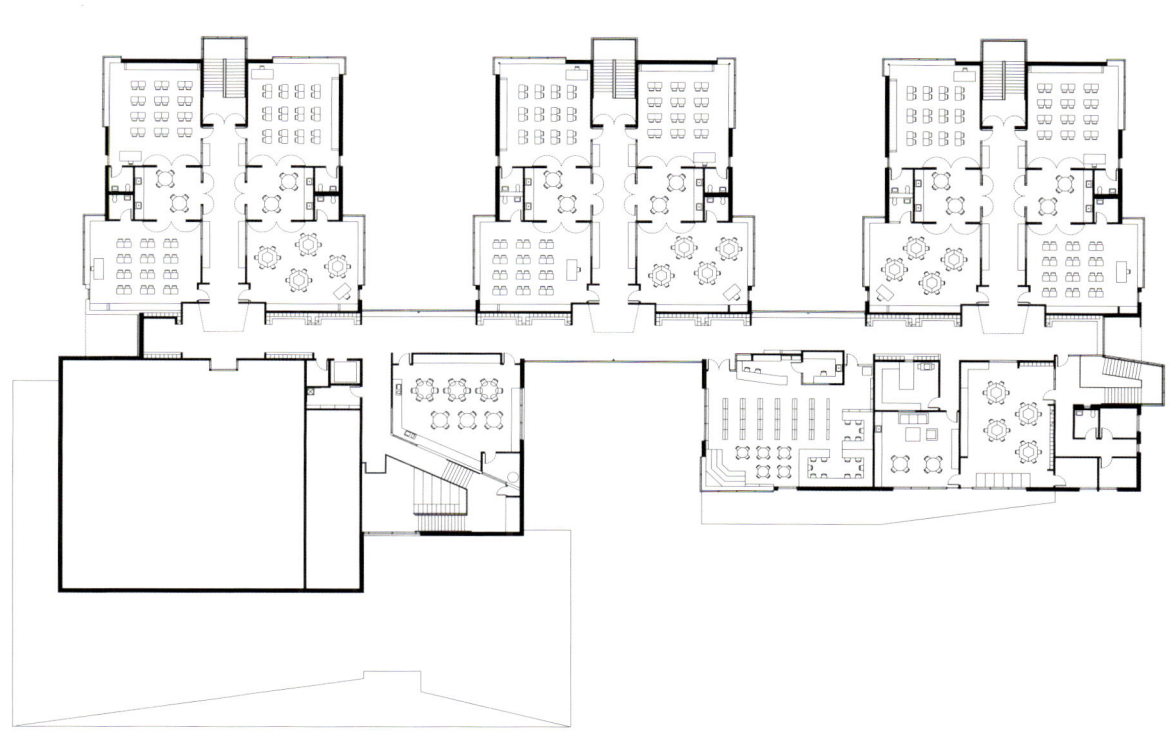

FEATHER RIVER ACADEMY

YUBA CITY, CALIFORNIA

This 24,600-square-foot school with 180 students from grades 7 to 12 serves children referred by the probation department, expelled by their local school, or homeless. Rather than design a single building with a parking lot in front and playfields in the back, this school expresses the county's mission statement, "Learning in Action." The layout of the campus disperses and interweaves the program, buildings, and open spaces across the entire site—an educational village. The site intermingles outdoor with indoor, athletics with classrooms, classrooms with administration, play areas with gardens, and multipurpose buildings with outdoor stage. The use of durable materials like colored concrete floors and textured concrete blocks are softened by redwood siding and custom wall murals in tile that depict the surrounding mountains. The folding roofs visually and experientially express the "Learning in Action" theme. The undulating roof overhangs create a changing journey, symbolic of the path of learning. (Architecture for Education.)

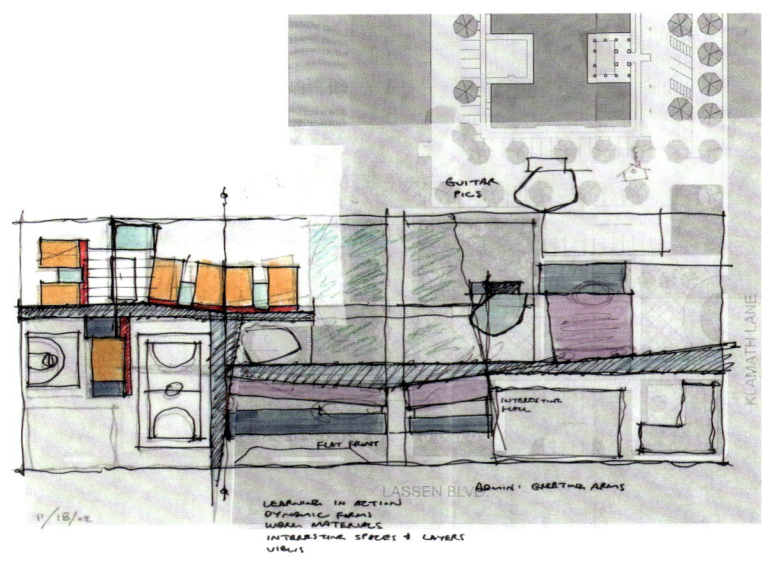

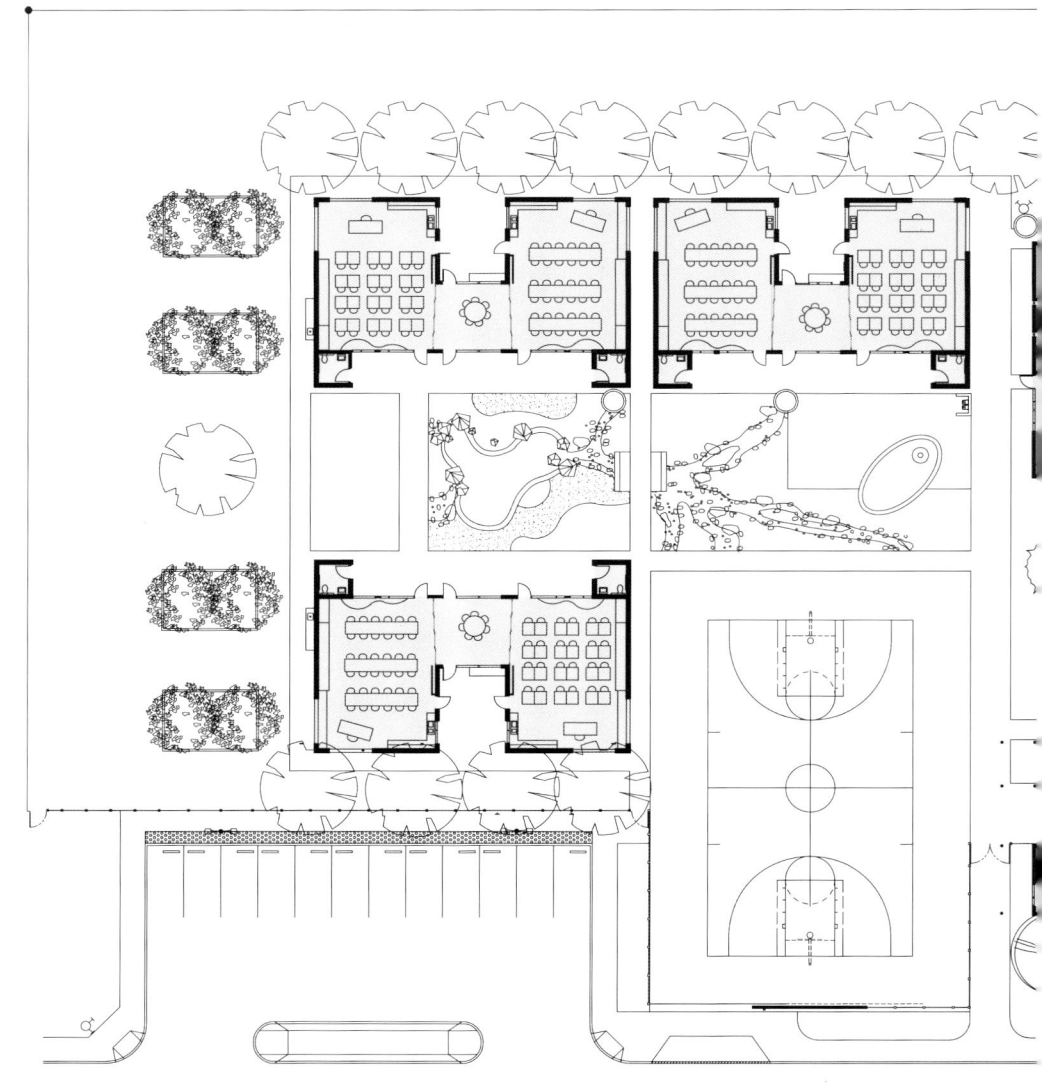

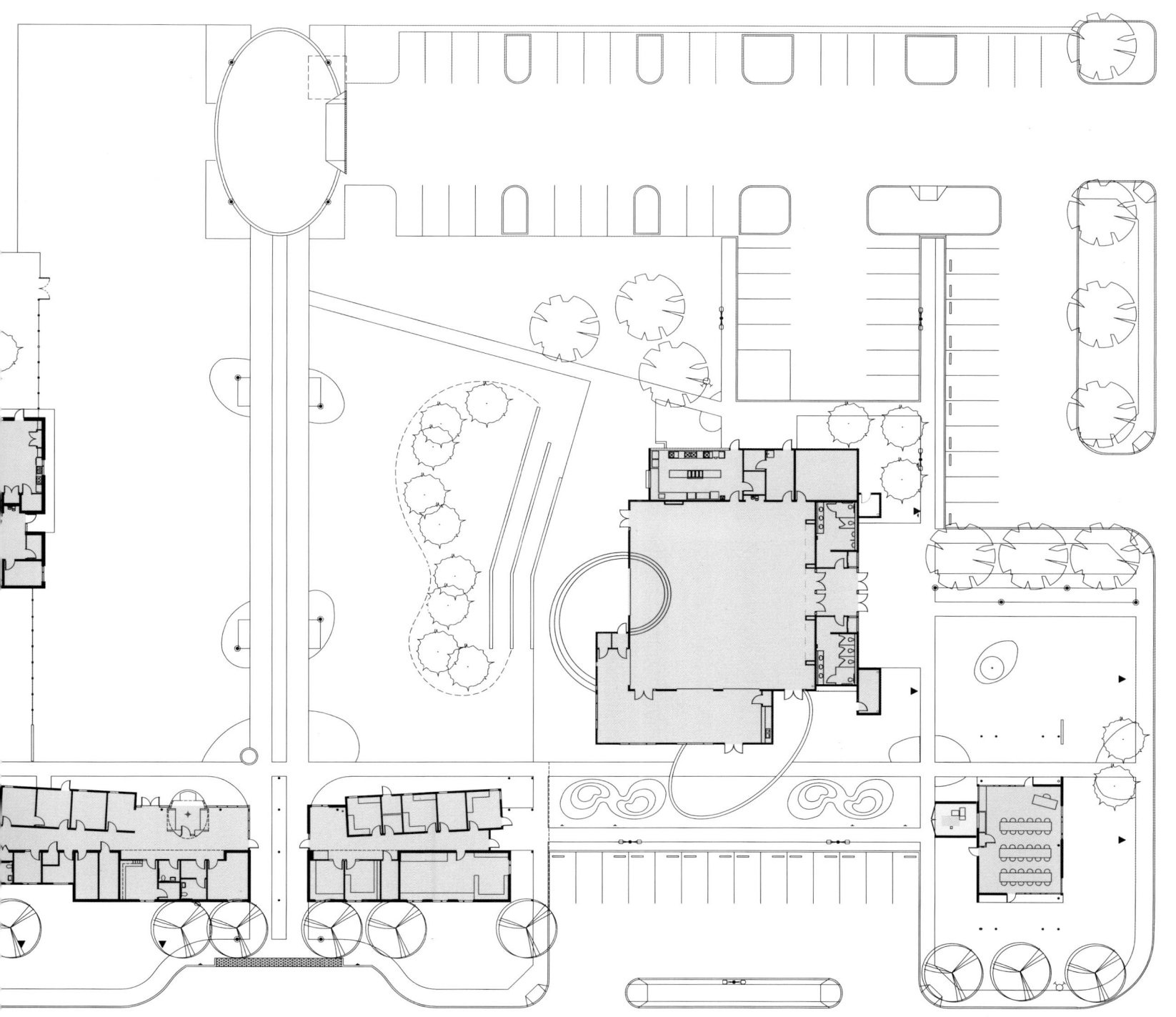

- ADMIN BR GATEWAY   660 × 240
- FORMAL PLAZA
- INFORMAL PLAZA

11/14 TH

SCHOOL CALL TO LARGER COMMUNITY

GARDENS — SPEC ED — HALF COURT / REC FIELD — PARKING

PARKING

REC. FIELD
SOUTH ROUND
DROP OFF

VISITOR PARKING
DROP OFF

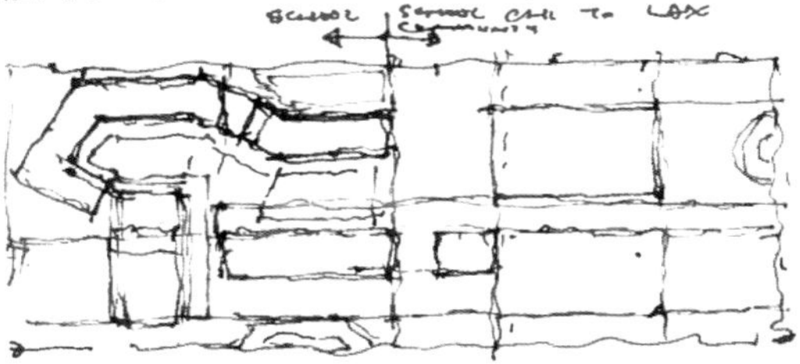

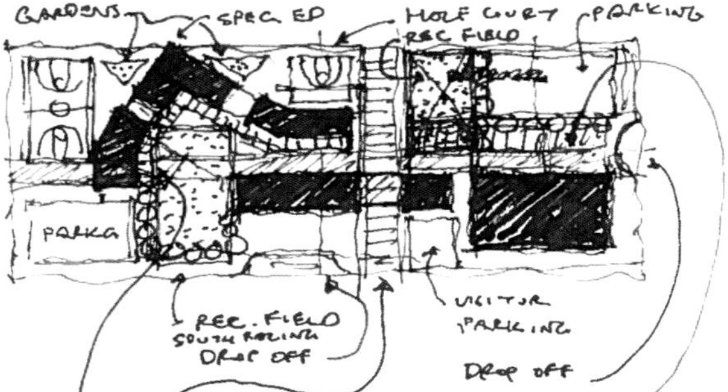

FORMAL PLAZA: CAFE STYLE SPILLOUT FROM M-P
KIT. SUPPORT FOR BBQ, SPORTS

ARCADE

CONNECTION TO OFFICE, EXTENSION, & CHILD CARE

FRONT PORCH & BACK PORCH

LAYERED SPACES INSIDE & OUTSIDE

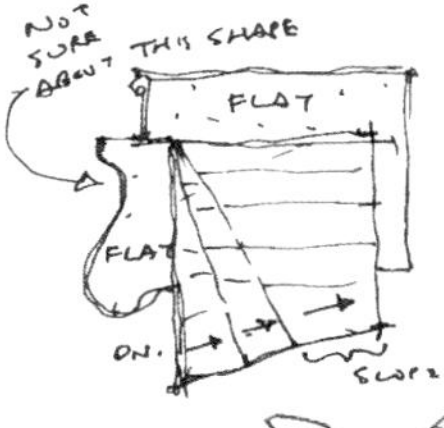

NOT SURE ABOUT THIS SHAPE

FLAT
FLAT
ON
SLOPE

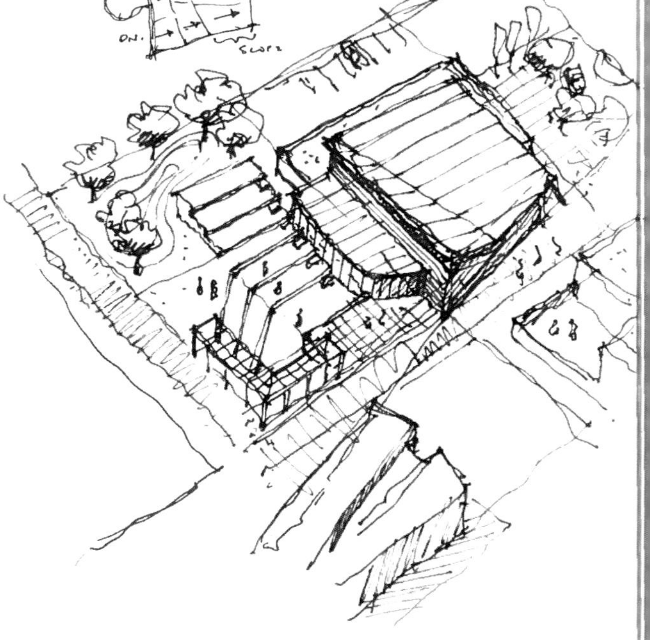

SAME BOX TRUSS THROUGHOUT,
FRAMING BUILT UP FOR FOLDING ROOF

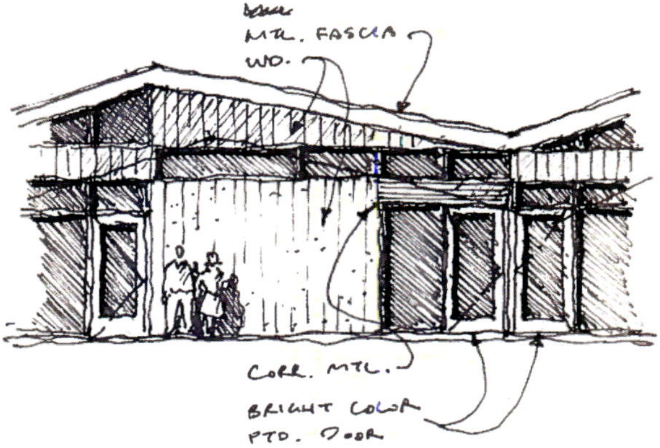

DANCING ROOF CLASSROOMS
①

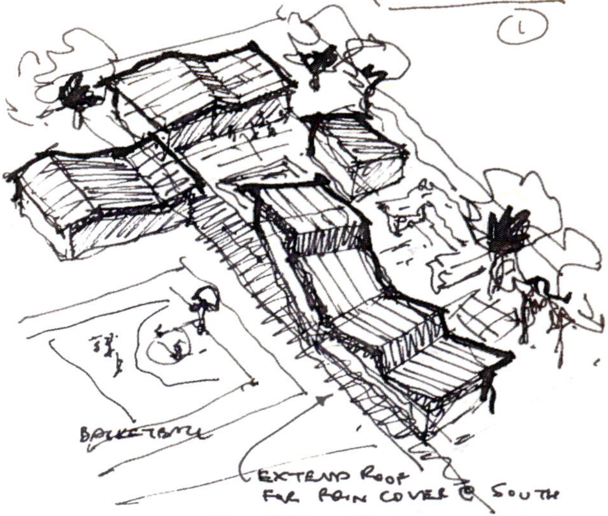

MTL. FASCIA
WD.

BASKETBALL

EXTEND ROOF
FOR RAIN COVER @ SOUTH

CLASSROOMS AND LEARNING ENVIRONMENTS
UNIFIED BY "LEARNING IN ACTION"
ROOF. DYNAMIC. FOLDING. IN MOTION.

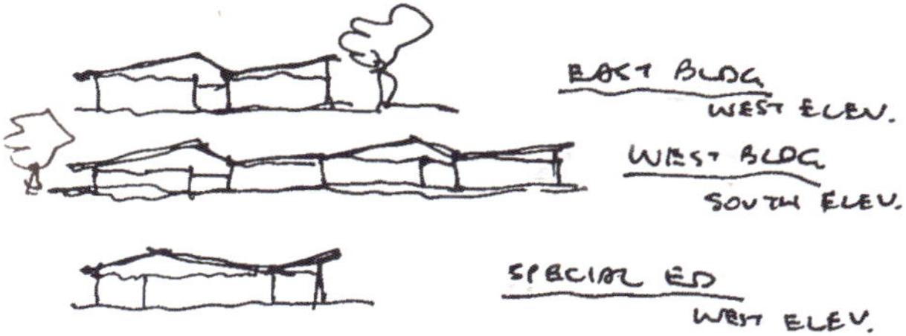

EAST BLDG
WEST ELEV.

WEST BLDG
SOUTH ELEV.

SPECIAL ED
WEST ELEV.

CORR. MTL.
BRIGHT COLOR
PTD. DOOR

GABLE = RESIDENTIAL
INTERPRETED

HERGET MIDDLE SCHOOL

AURORA, ILLINOIS

A new 113,000-square-foot school for 850 students on a 38-acre rural property resembles an assembly of modern farmhouses. Rather than the long, narrow hallway seen in most schools the Herget Middle School's main circulation is the library, tech center, life skills lab, and process labs, contained within a hall 60 feet wide and 30 feet tall. Six neighborhoods of classrooms focus on six different academic themes. Through a roll-up barn door, each classroom connects to their resource area—a small community family room. The school district's design theme for the project is "The Heartland," which is expressed through industrial and agricultural materials, including fieldstone, corrugated and standing seam metal, brick, and wood. Building forms and rooflines recall the old farmhouses and barns that once stood on the property. The design allows for educational partnerships with the nearby Aurora University and the local YMCA. (Architecture for Education, with associate architect, Cordogan, Clark & Associates.)

2/11/03 IN AURORA
NEW MIDDLE SCHOOL
SHOULD BE ONE BIG ROOF
FOR ONE CENTRAL SPACE
EXTANDED
YMCA
MORE FARM LIKE
TOO MUCH LIKE FRAME
41
21
17
14
0

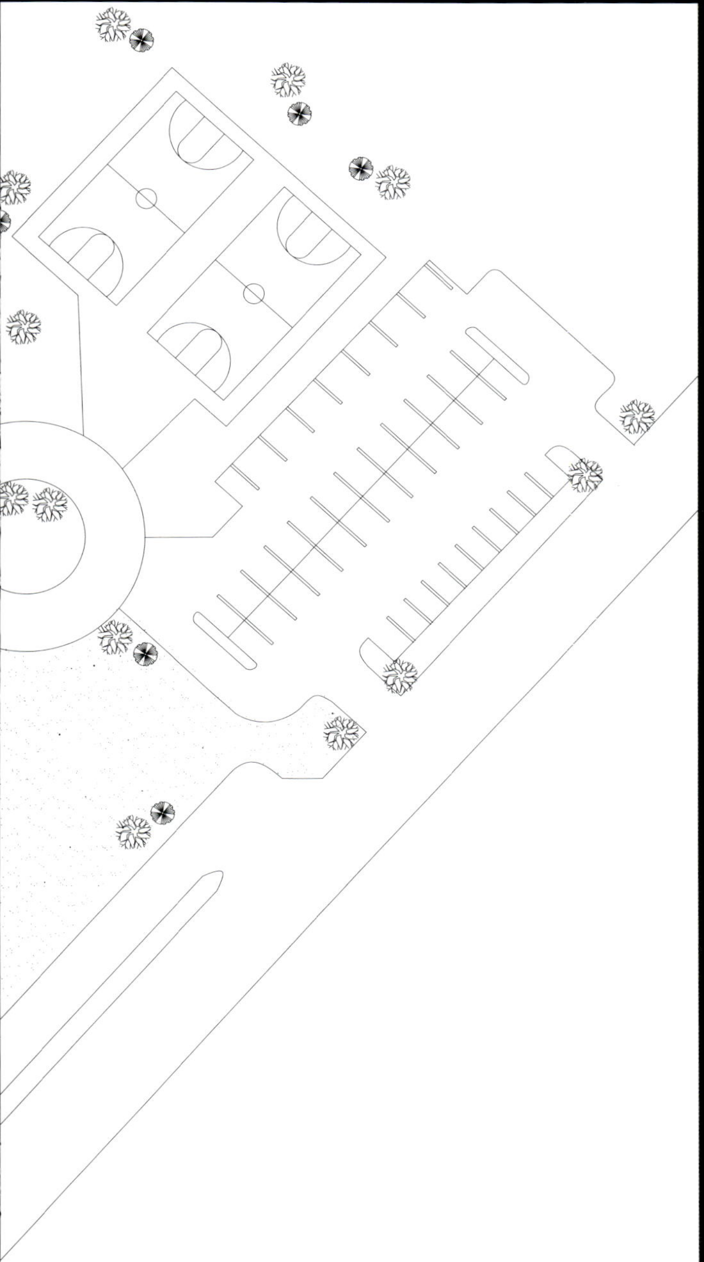

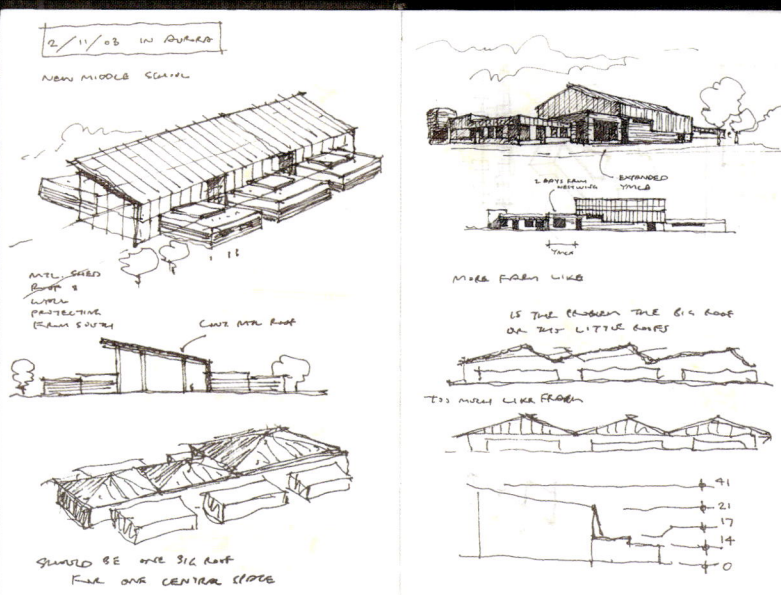

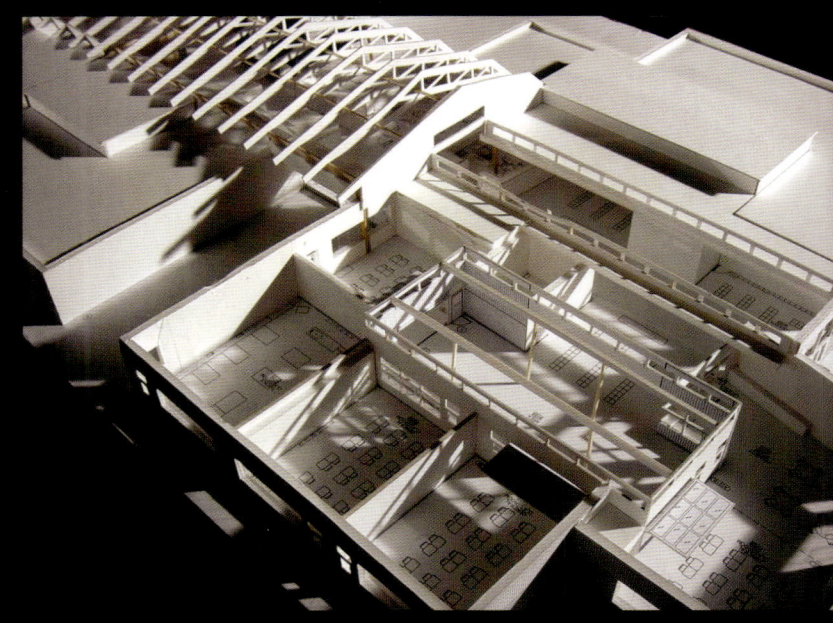

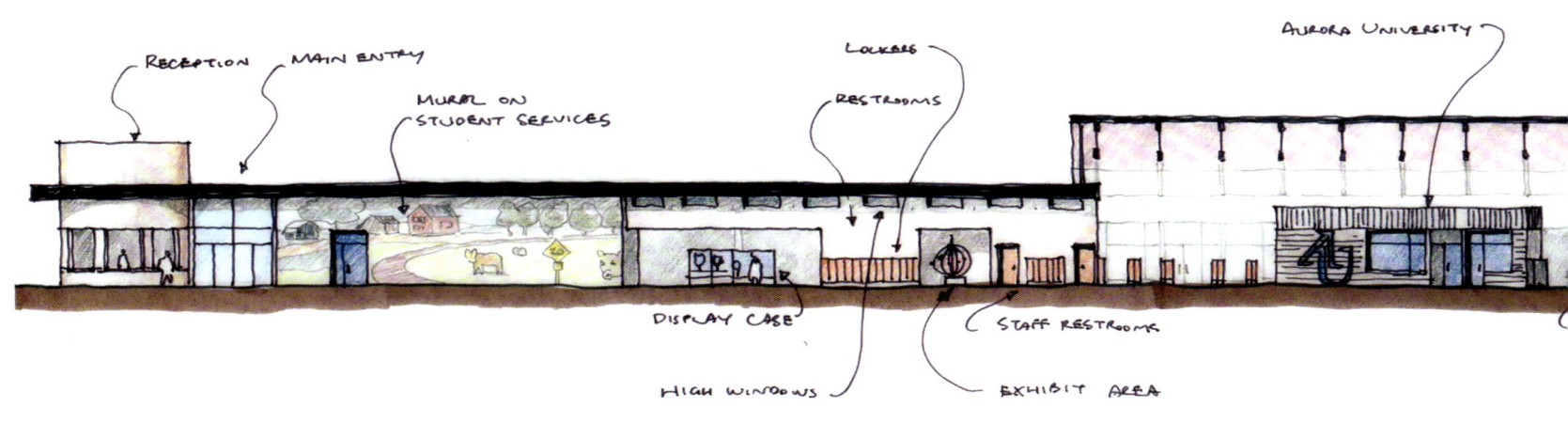
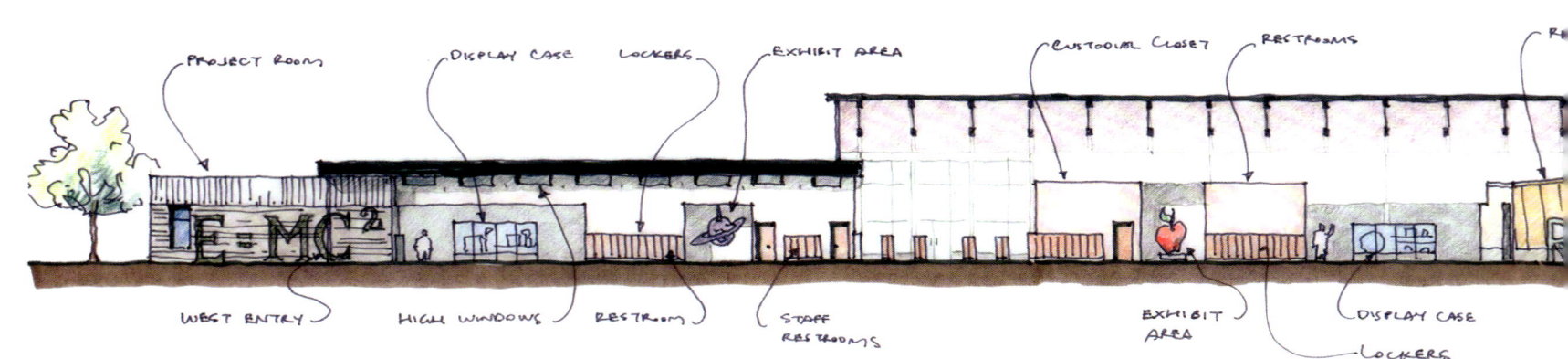

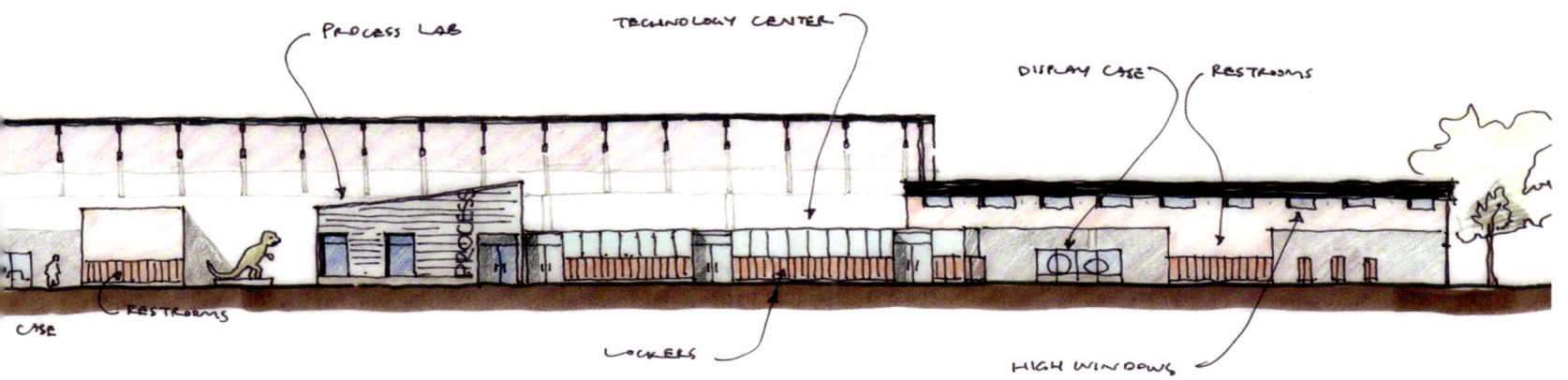

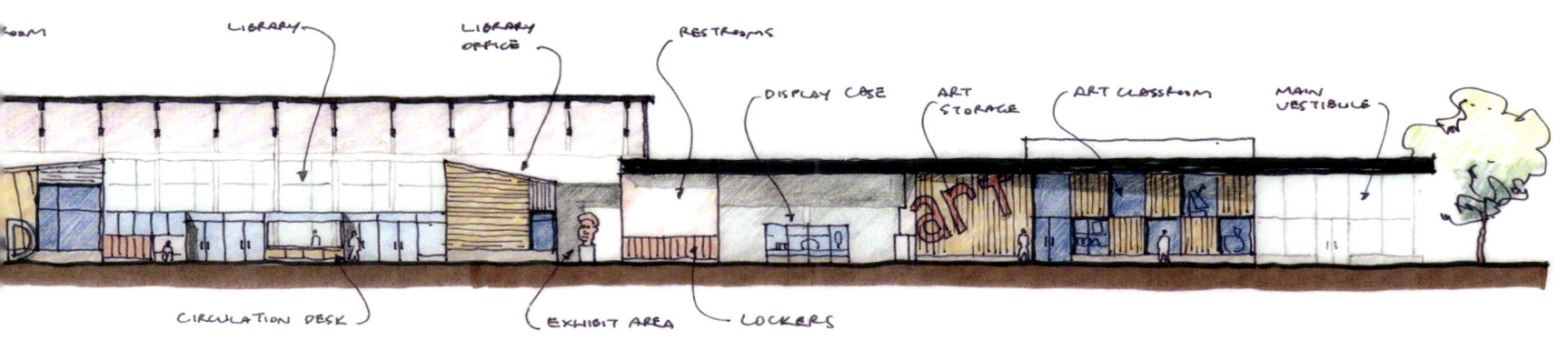

BEL AIR PRESBYTERIAN PRESCHOOL

LOS ANGELES, CALIFORNIA

This 23,000-square-foot preschool campus is located in the Santa Monica Mountains. It comprises 11 classrooms, five learning yards, separate pavilions for library, music, and art, a central courtyard, multipurpose buildings, and an administration building. The design suggests a village of small-scaled buildings with cement plaster and cedar exterior, covered walkways, big roof overhangs, and bamboo classroom flooring. Students experience native landscape and specimen trees, butterfly and hummingbird gardens, water features, an amphitheater, and shade structures, all surrounded by mountain vistas.

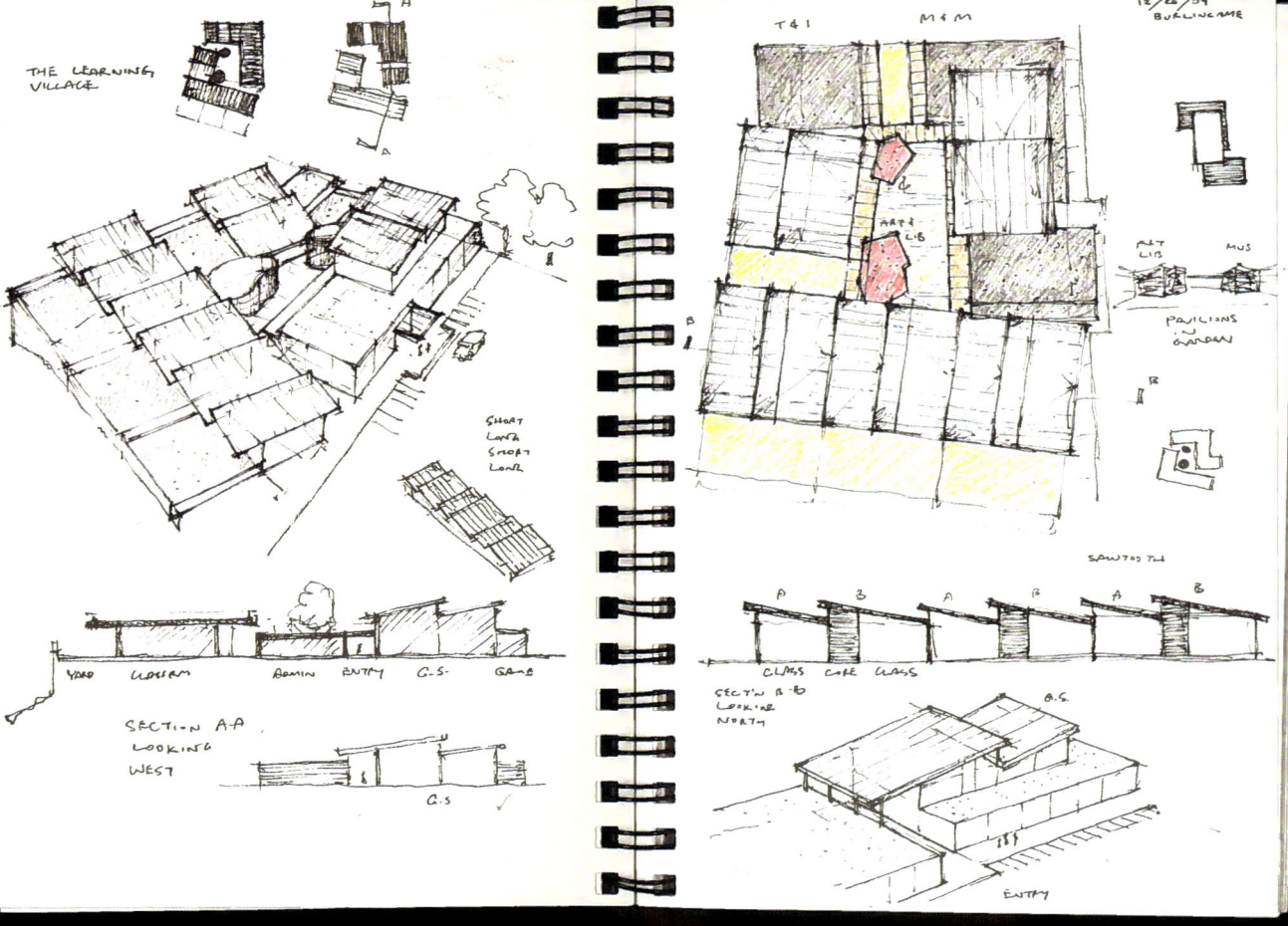

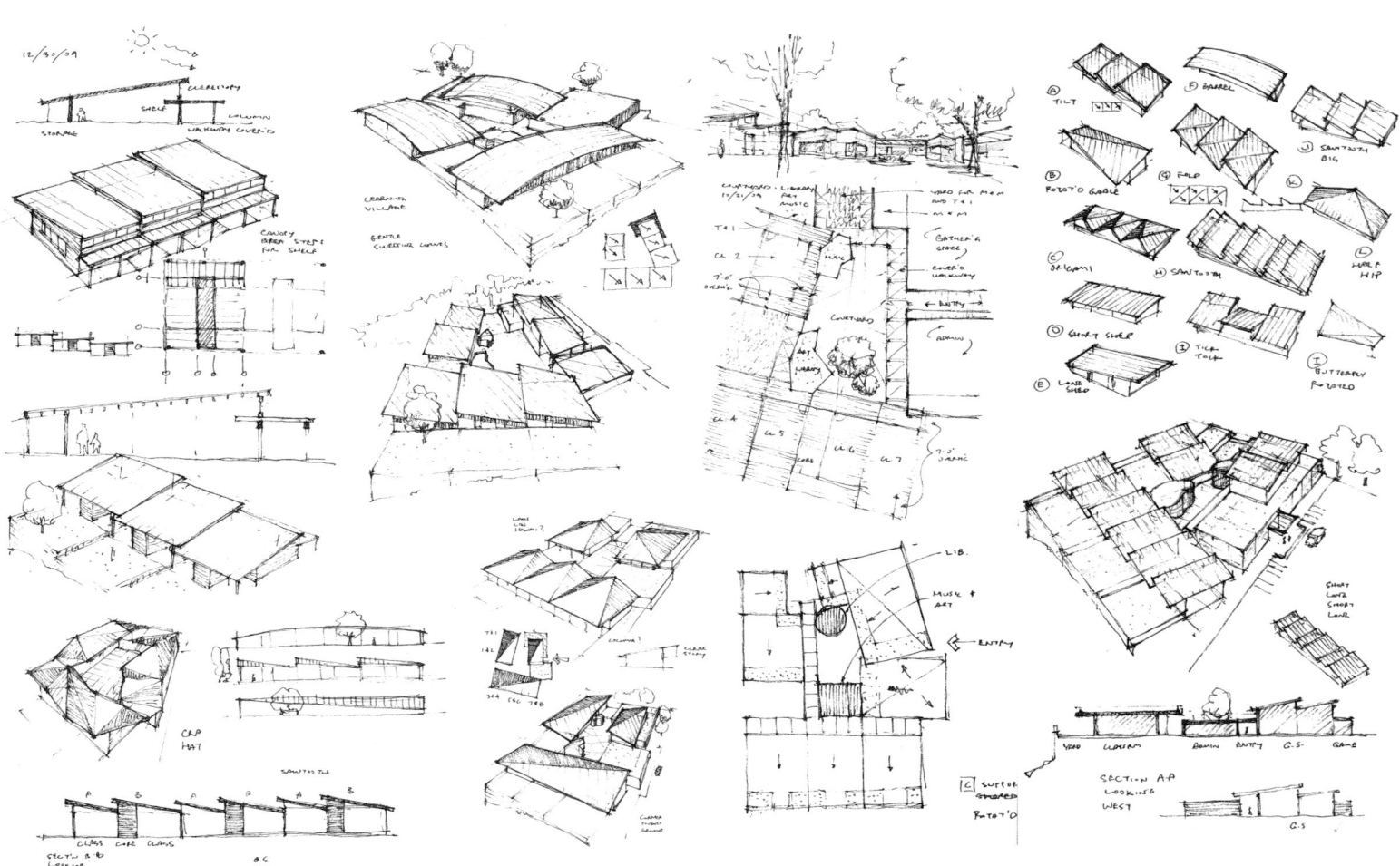

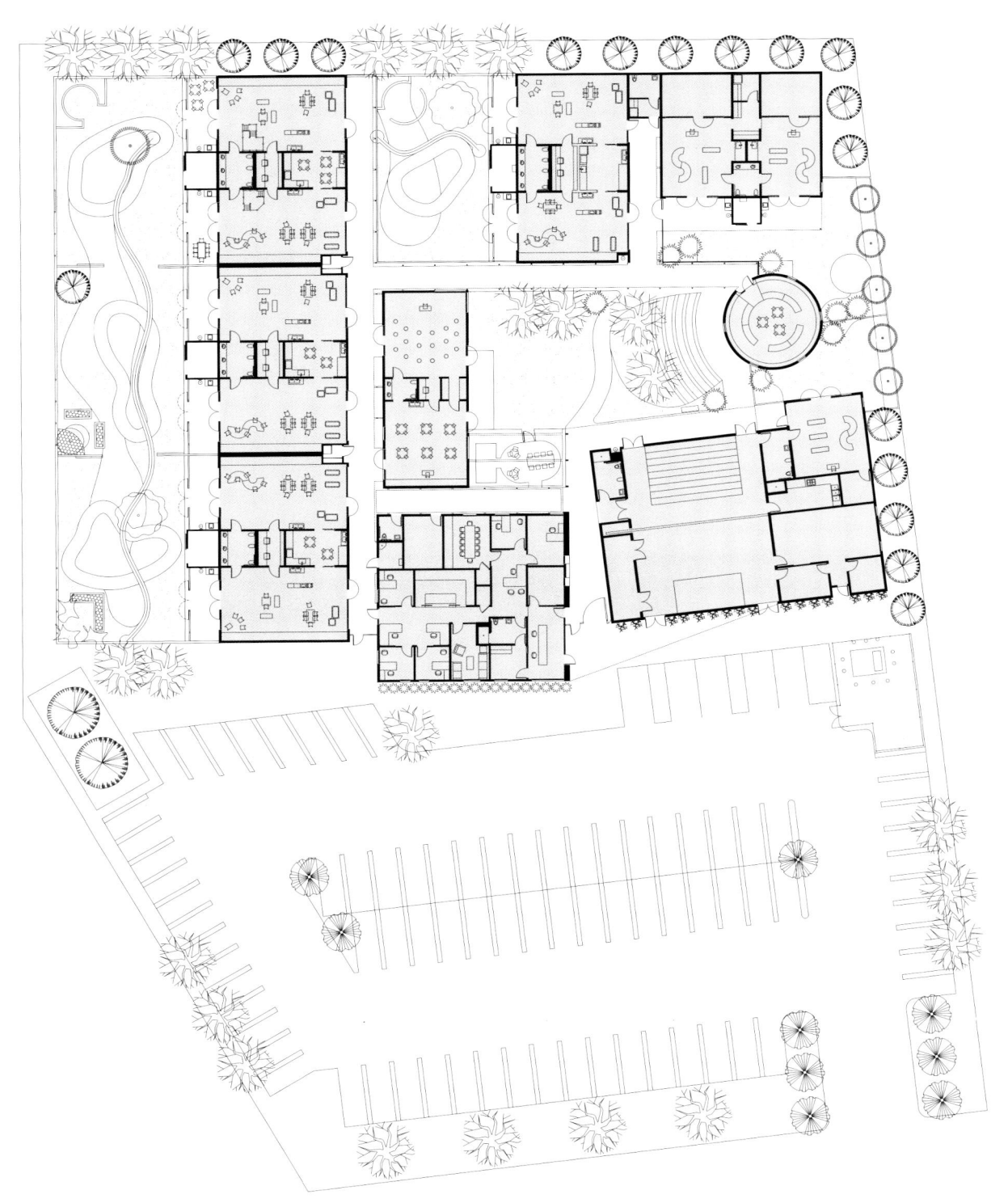

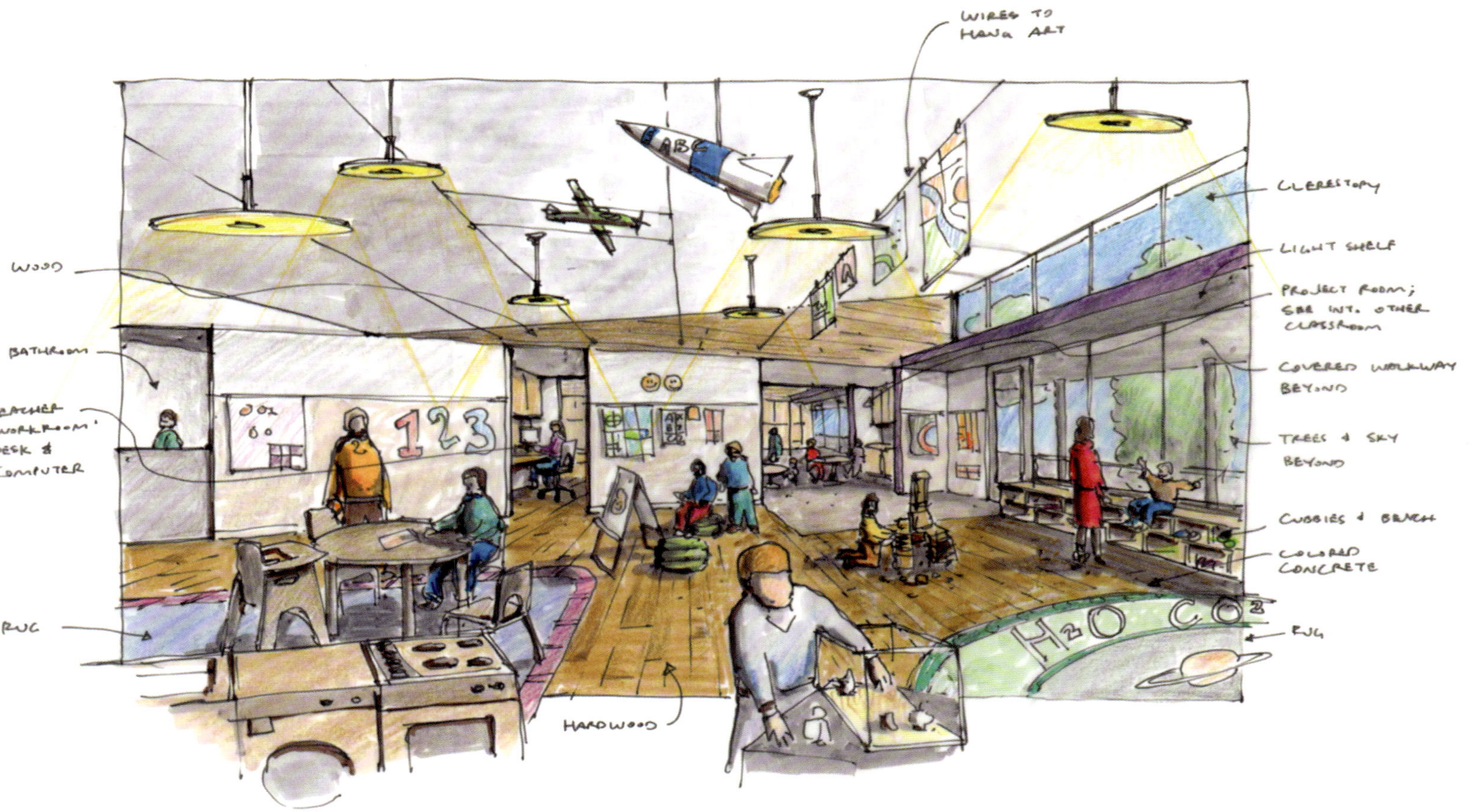
WIRES TO HANG ART
CLERESTORY
LIGHT SHELF
PROJECT ROOM; SEE INT. OTHER CLASSROOM
COVERED WALKWAY BEYOND
TREES & SKY BEYOND
CUBBIES & BENCH
COLORED CONCRETE
RUG
HARDWOOD
RUG
TEACHER WORKROOM: DESK & COMPUTER
BATHROOM
WOOD
ABC
123

123

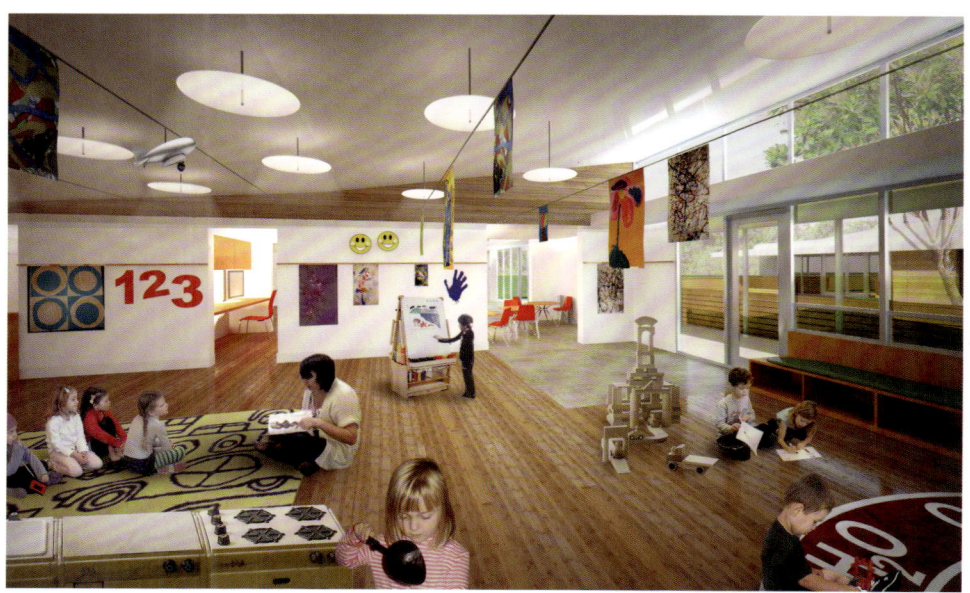

EAT

CHAYA DOWNTOWN

LOS ANGELES, CALIFORNIA

A comprehensive experience of architecture, interiors, landscape, furniture design, lighting design, graphics, and music programming—this 8,000-square-foot, 210-seat restaurant is enriched by a diversity of art works, including a mural by Japanese artist Ajioka on Hinoki-style cypress planks, a Venetian-influenced backlit mirror proscenium at the bar, a solid walnut slab community table, red lacquer details at the sushi bar, woven brass wire mesh screens, Calacatta white marble, hand-troweled plaster, and a feature art piece by London-based light artist Stuart Haygarth. Two glass building additions complement the corporate tower: the main entrance and a private dining room. Floating above the glass rooms and the outdoor space is a 90-foot-long roof canopy. The underside of the canopy is made of Spanish brass panels, serving as a glowing sign from across public plaza. At the edge of the patio, dining booths are carved into the hedges.

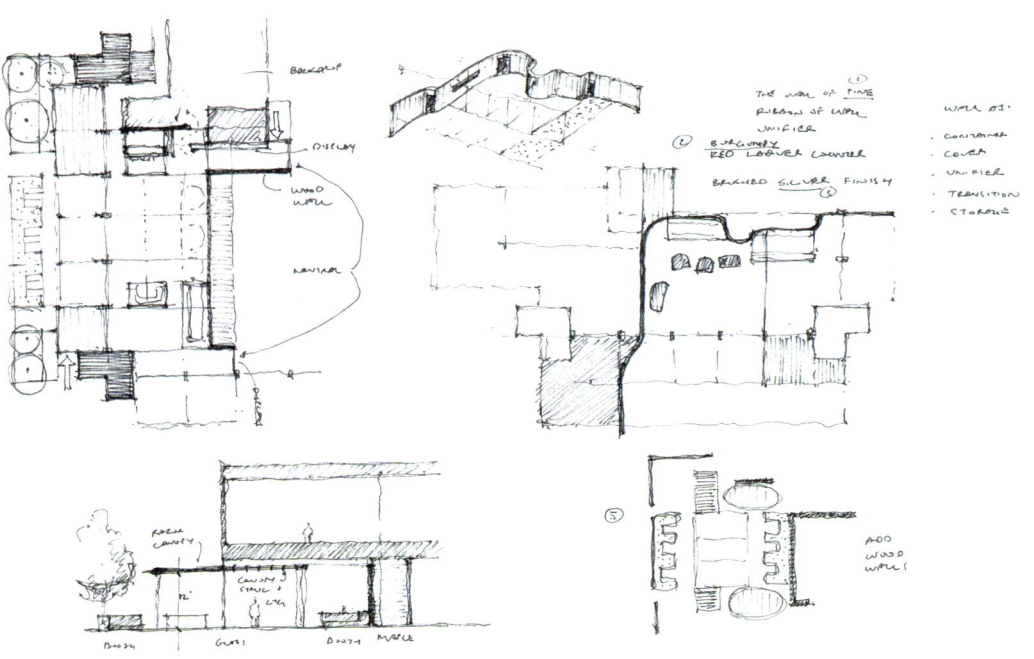

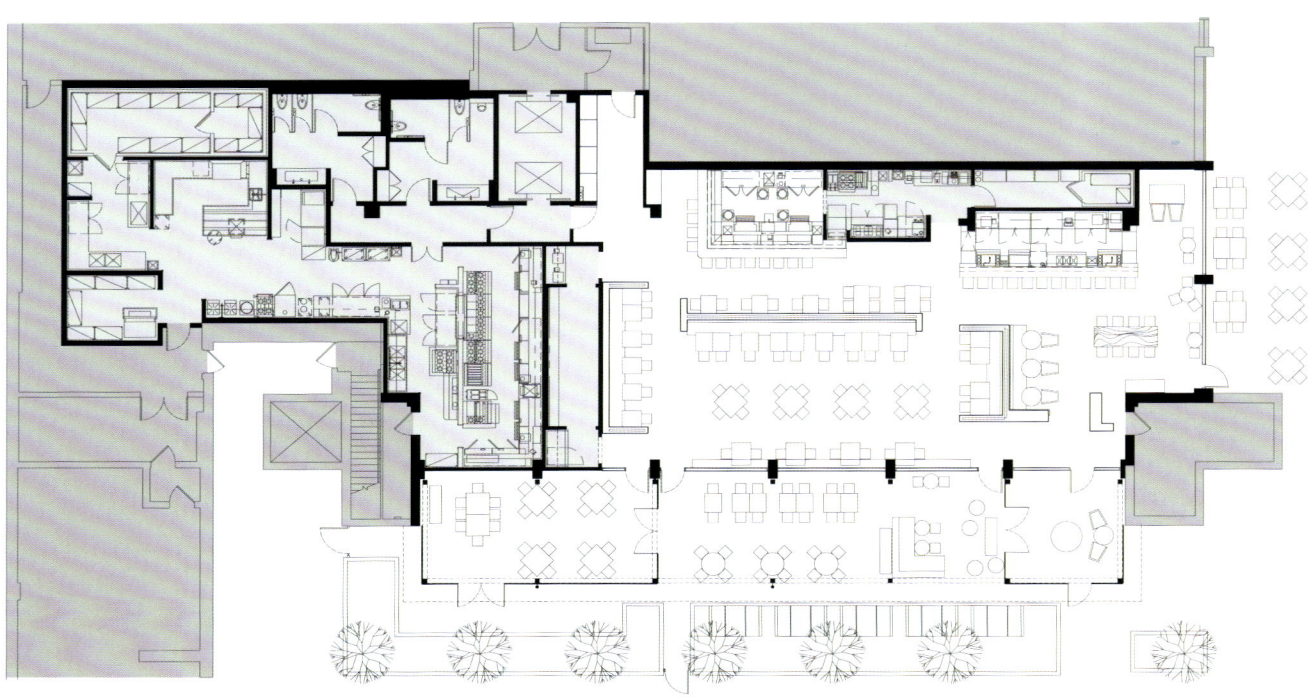

MENDOCINO FARMS

LOS ANGELES, MARINA DEL REY
AND WEST HOLLYWOOD, CALIFORNIA

For six completed locations of a casual restaurant chain, the craft of making sandwiches inspires the architecture, interiors, and furniture design. They range in size from 2,000 to 7,000 square feet with 50 to 130 seats, and the deli-style marketplaces are characterized by eclectic and whimsical compositions. On an economical budget, fine materials such as walnut planks, stainless steel, and Carrara marble are contrasted with a polished concrete floor, vintage ceiling fans, chalkboards, and reused industrial items. The signature, floating ceiling is made of antique, stamped tin panels, and the custom designed furniture is comprised of wood, off-the-shelf piping, galvanized metal, and blackened raw steel. Artistic installations include chandeliers made from 1,600 wood clothespins on wire frames, the owner's quotes water-jet cut out of metal panels, chalk board walls with a vintage meat scale, vaudeville lit signage, a tree growing out of the community table, and walls of artificial grass.

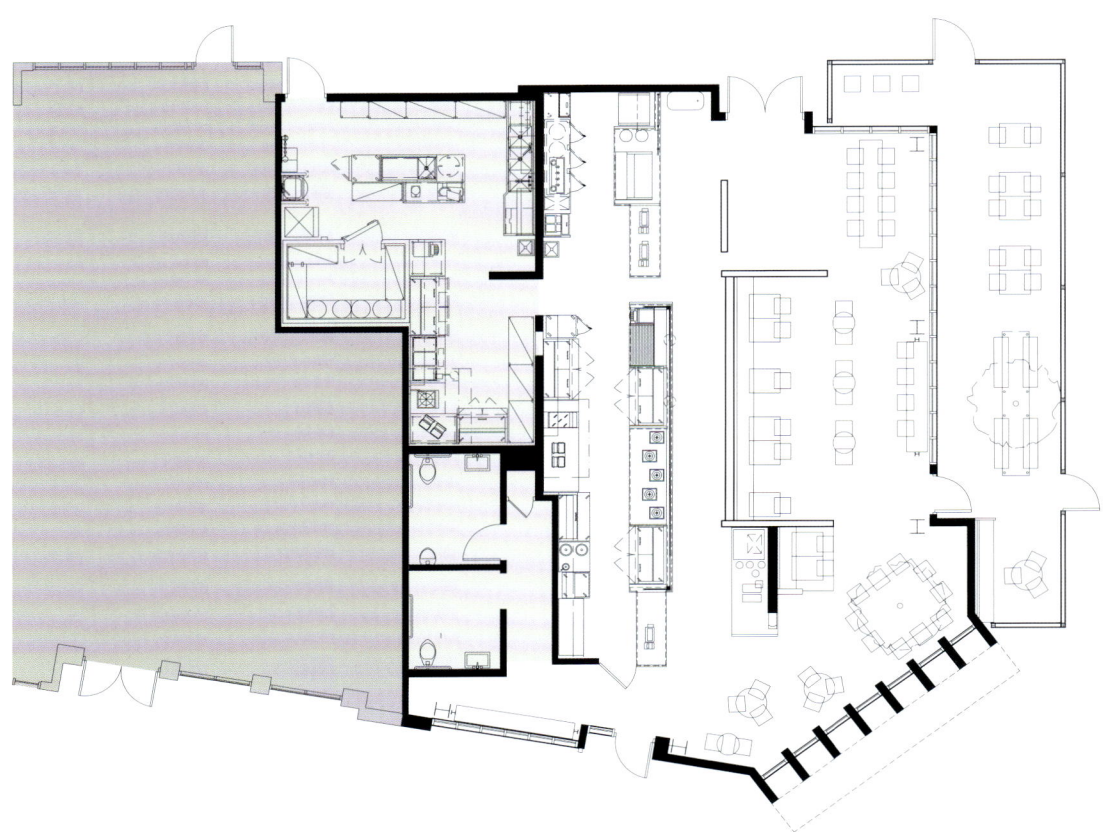

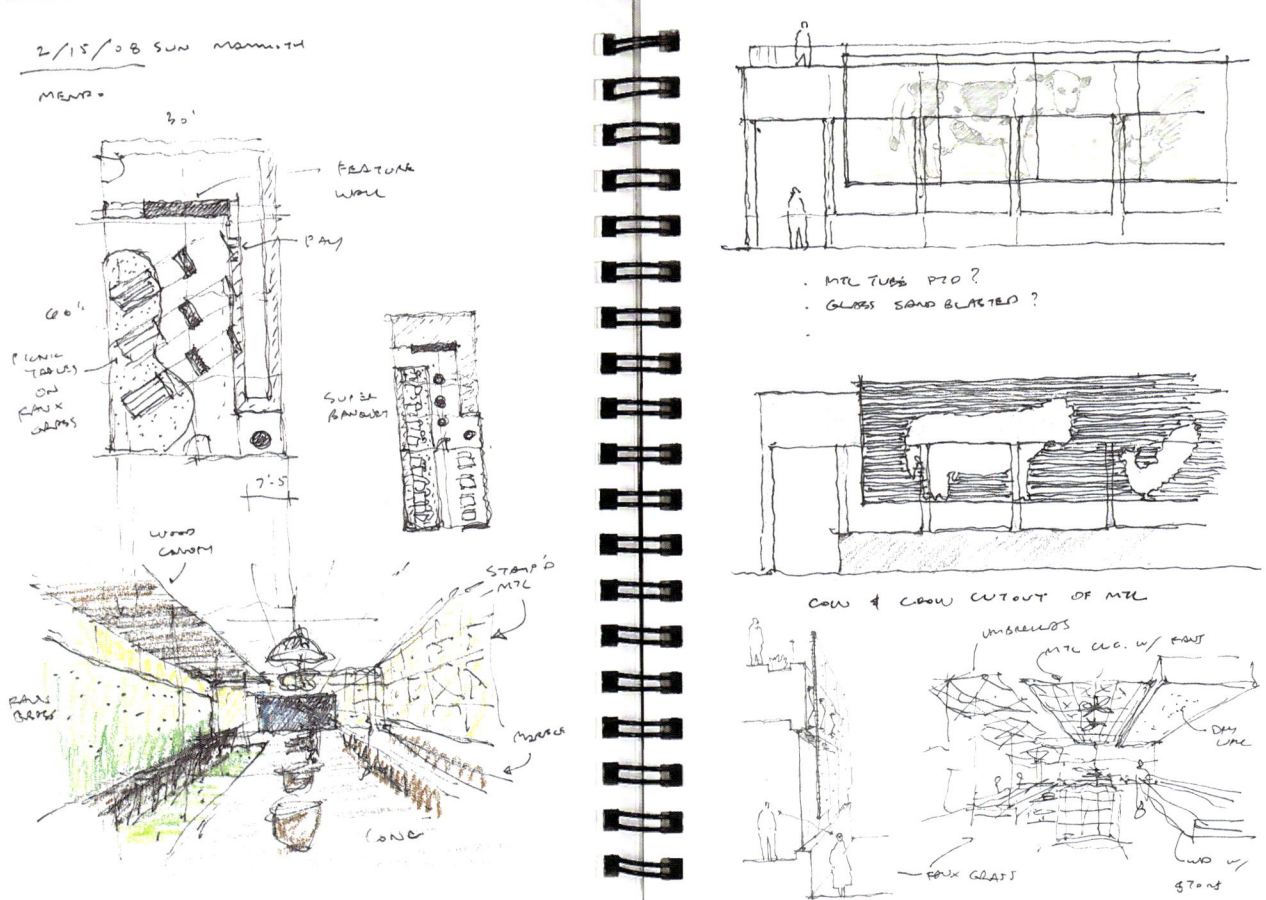

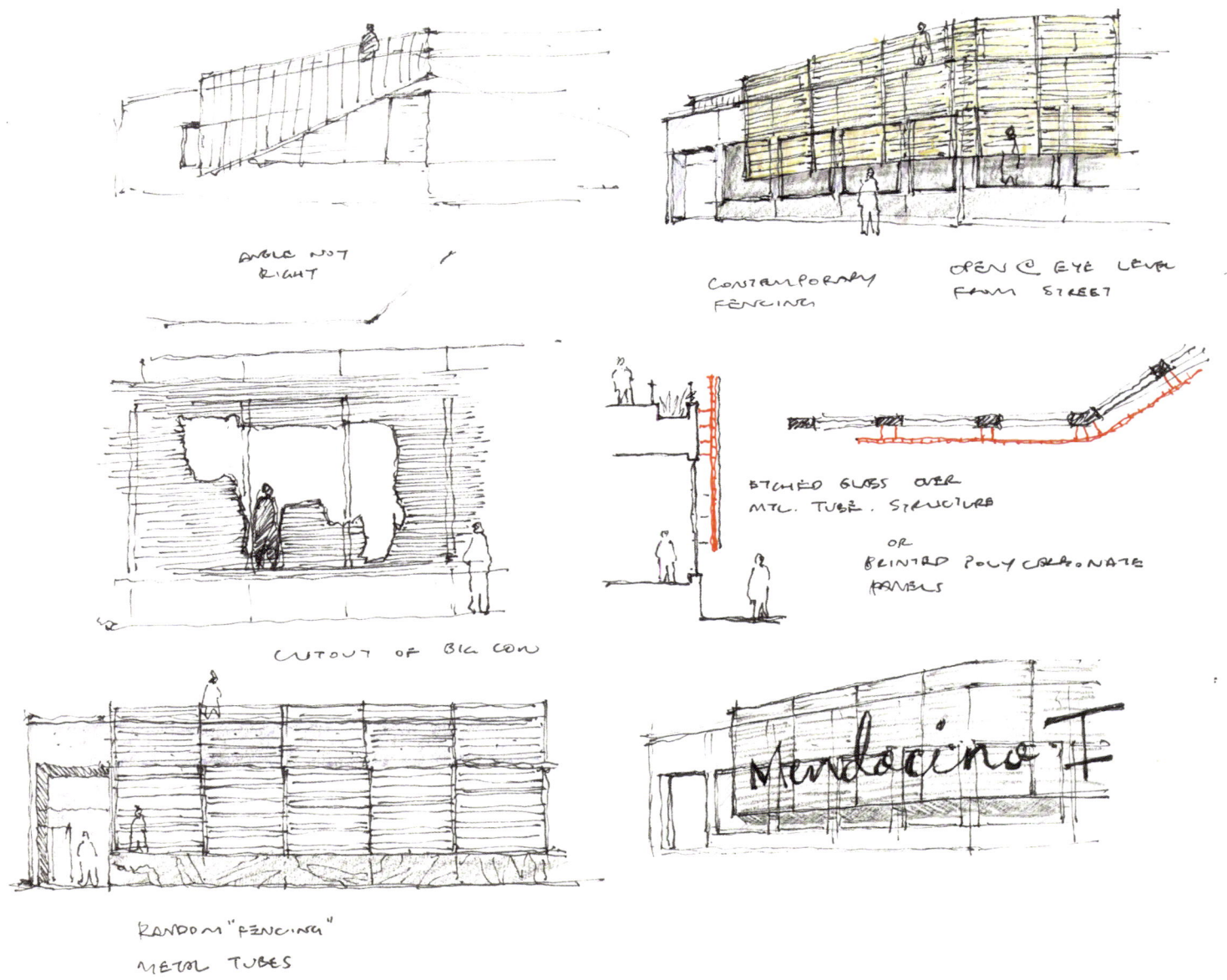

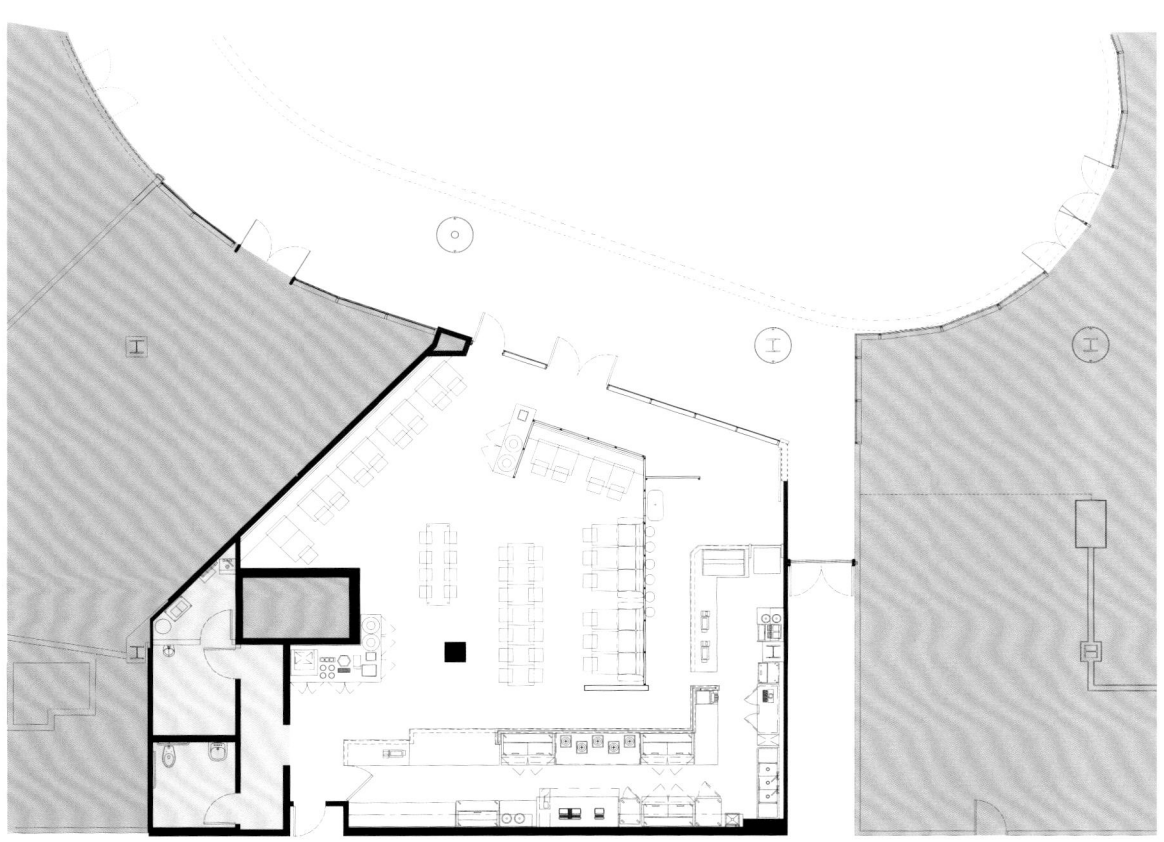

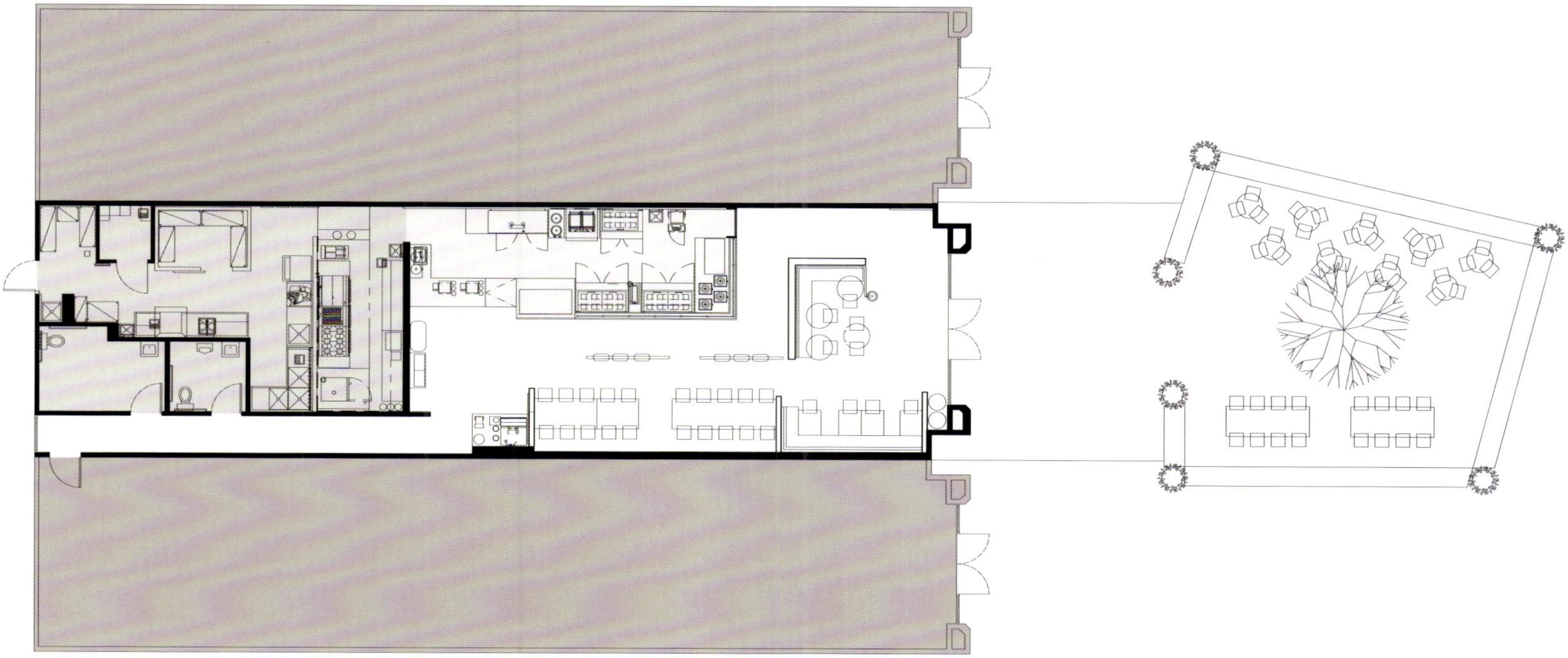

MENDOCINO FARMS
sandwich market

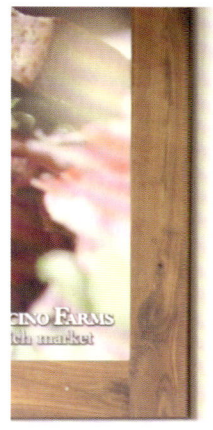

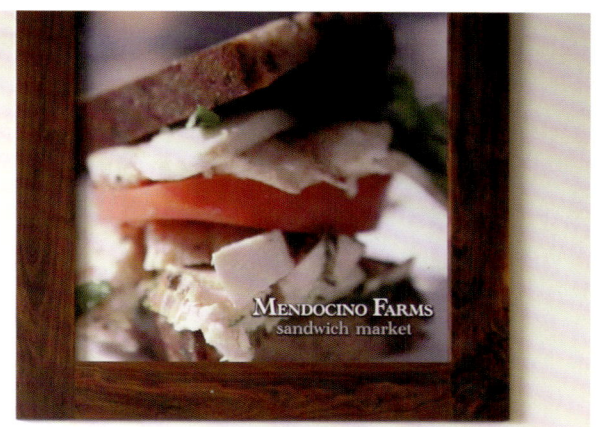

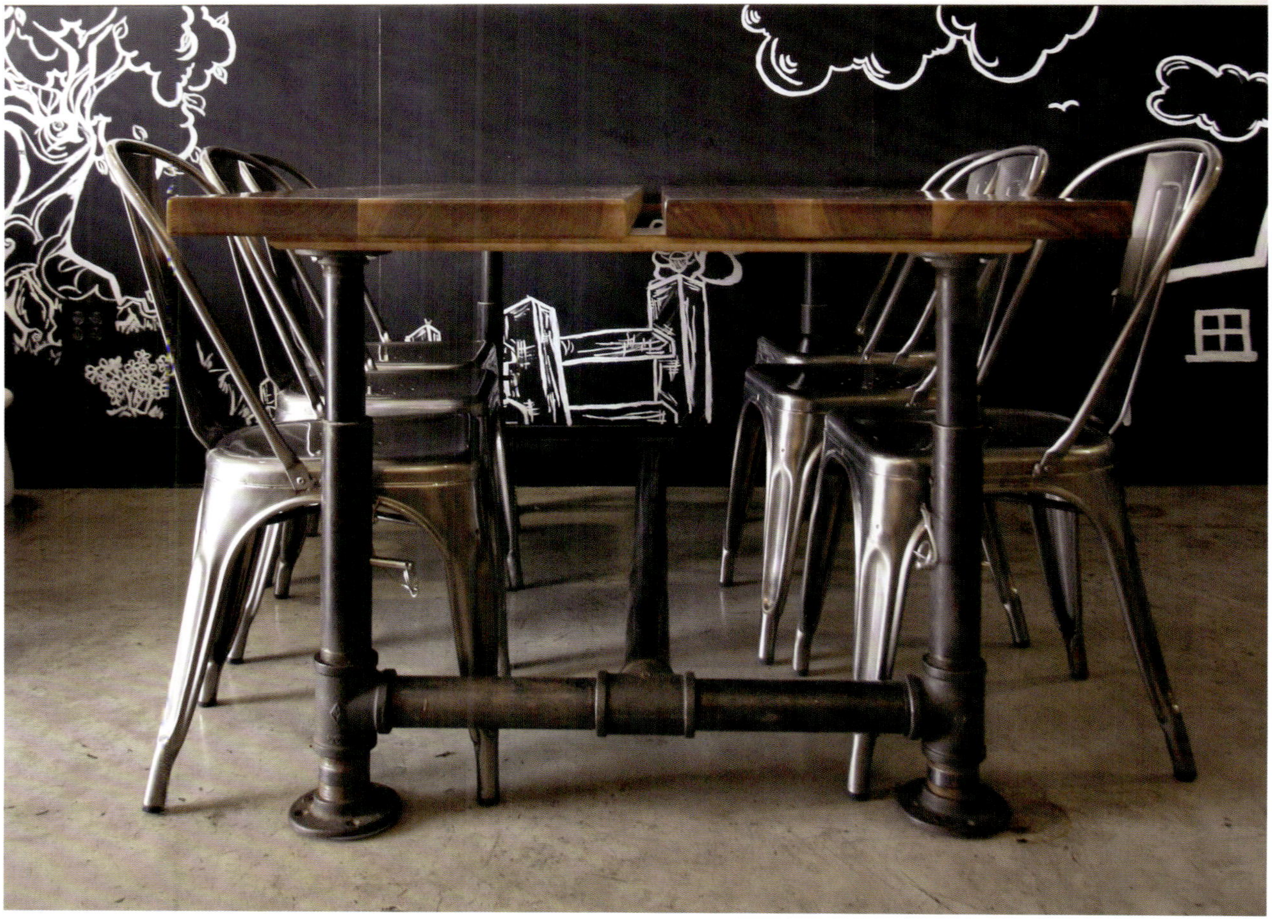

DIN TAI FUNG
THE AMERICANA AT BRAND

GLENDALE, CALIFORNIA

The architecture captures the old world of Asian hand-crafted artistry with modern materials and methods of fabrication. The 7,000-square-foot project comprises 160 seats. Inspiration comes from the exhibition dumpling kitchen—a motif of circles derived from the bamboo steamers in which the handmade dumplings are served. Circles are water-jet cut from white oak ceiling panels, and laser cut from the same wood and laminated between two layers of glass. Other features include heavily grained oak planks, brass inlay Chinese characters, Juno limestone, and black porcelain flooring. The furniture is custom designed in oak with orange suede and forest green leather.

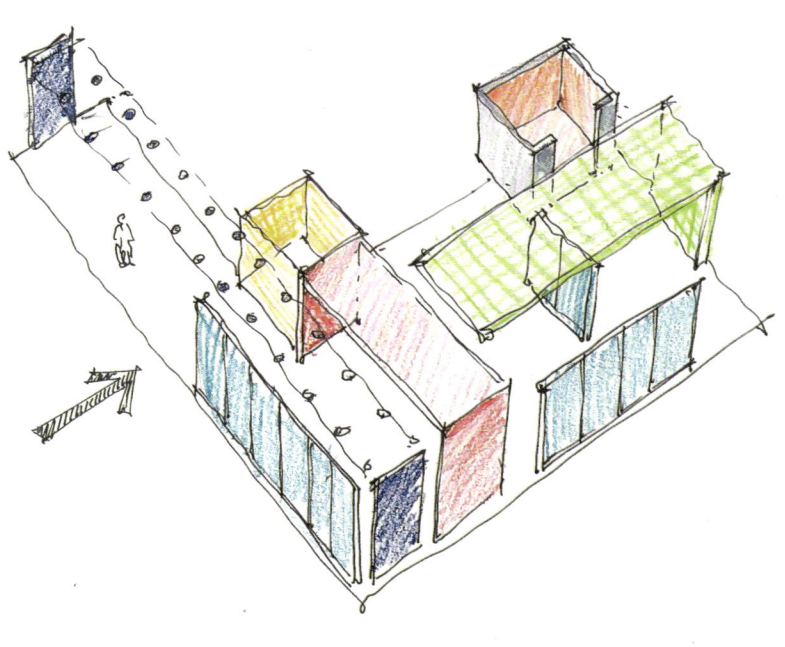

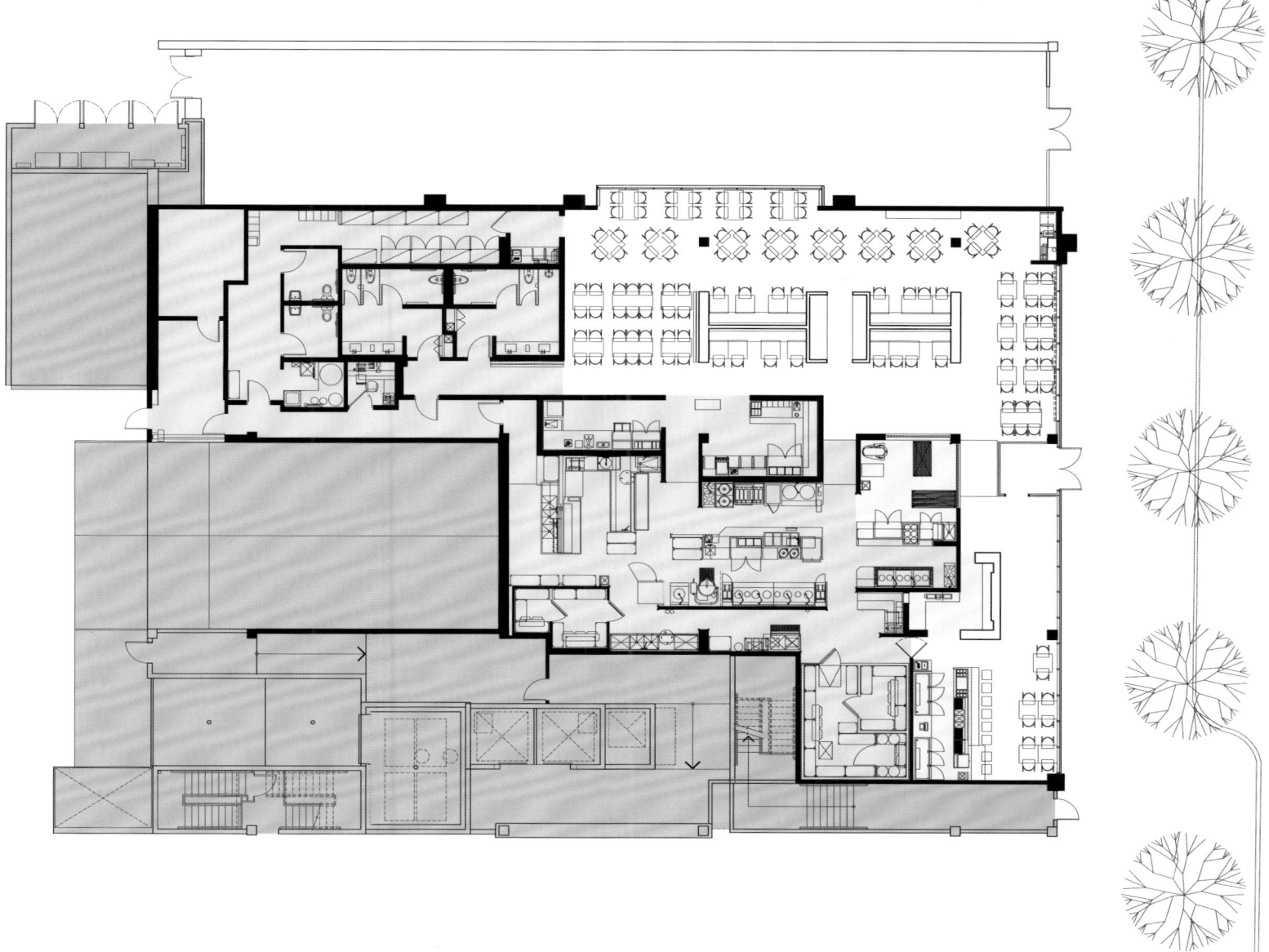

DIN TAI FUNG
SOUTH COAST PLAZA

COSTA MESA, CALIFORNIA

An 8,000-square-foot restaurant containing 175 seats includes a bar and lounge with custom-designed walnut stools, a casual dining area walled in honed sandstone with skylight boxes milled from walnut plywood, a ground-up grand dining room with a James Turrell-inspired elliptical dome, and an outdoor patio under a steel canopy. The shaped plaster ceiling at the exhibition kitchen echoes the restored 1960s sculptural entry pavilion.

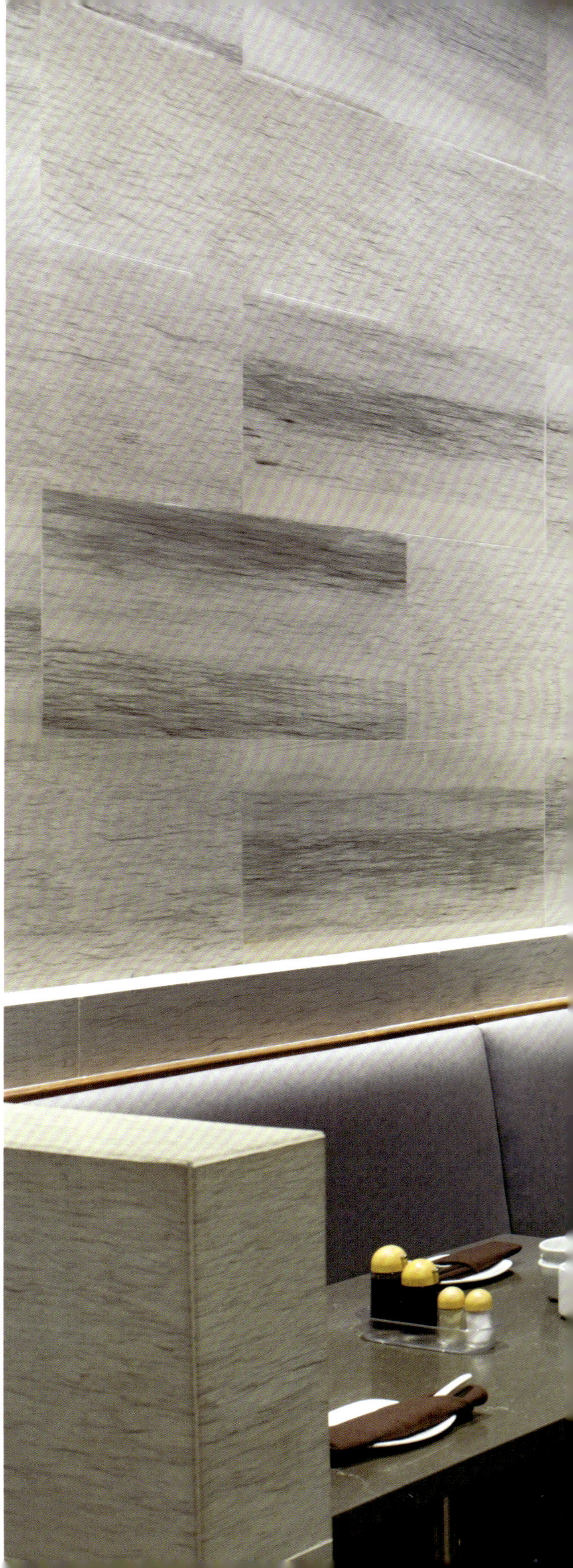

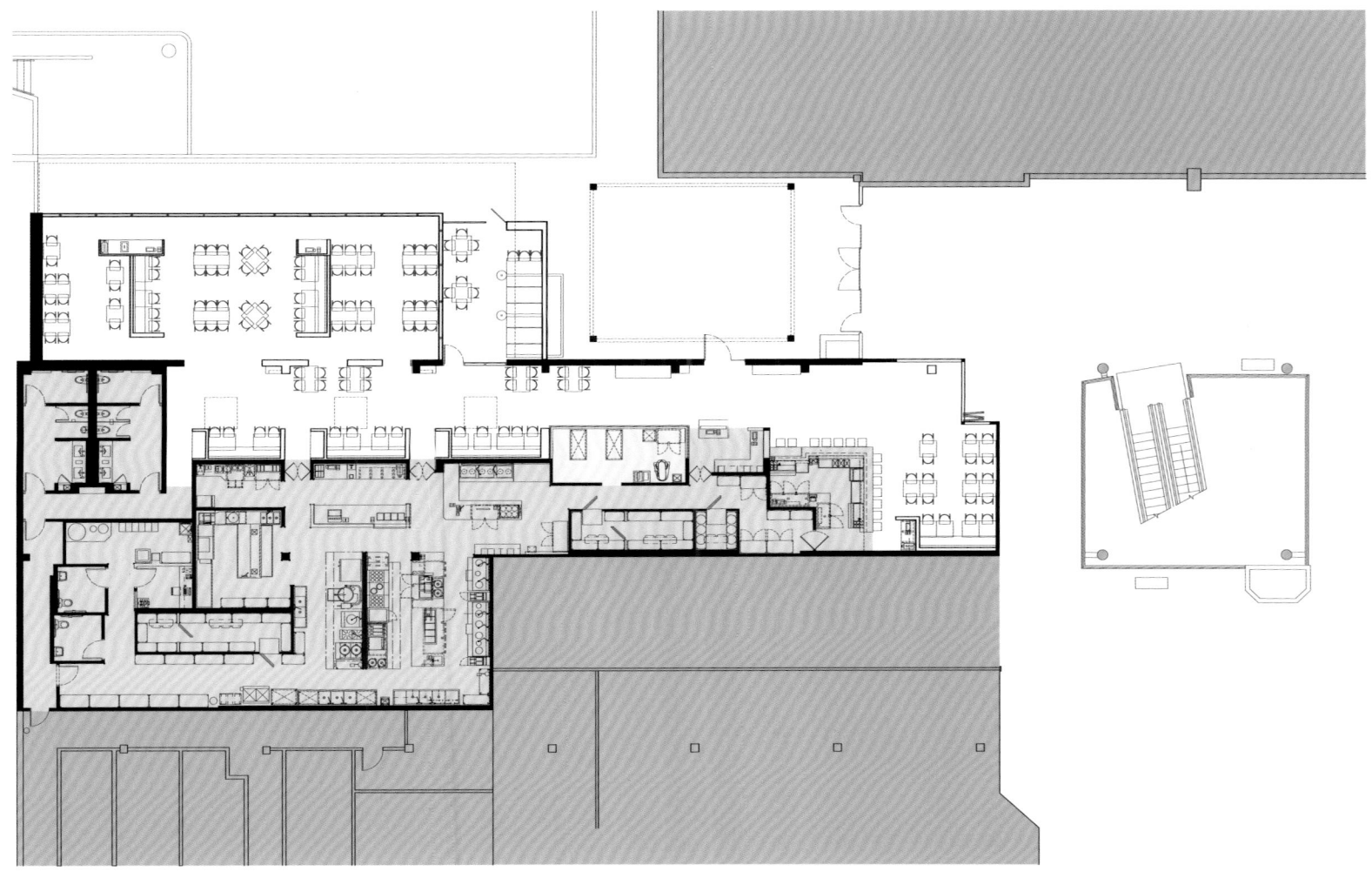

VOSGES HAUT-CHOCOLAT

BEVERLY HILLS, CALIFORNIA

In a retail space only 14 feet wide and 110 feet in length, a journey of three experiences explores the culture of gourmet chocolates. The first experience is for arrival and gathering, with its café setting and a sensory installation displaying the story of chocolate around the world. The second is the marketplace—merchandising and sales. The high ceiling is hand painted and groin-vaulted, contrasting with the intimacy of the entry area. The third is the "Chocolate Theater," where visitors seated at a community table watch the chefs at work. Linking the three experiences are Moroccan arches hand cast and carved by artisans in Marrakesh.

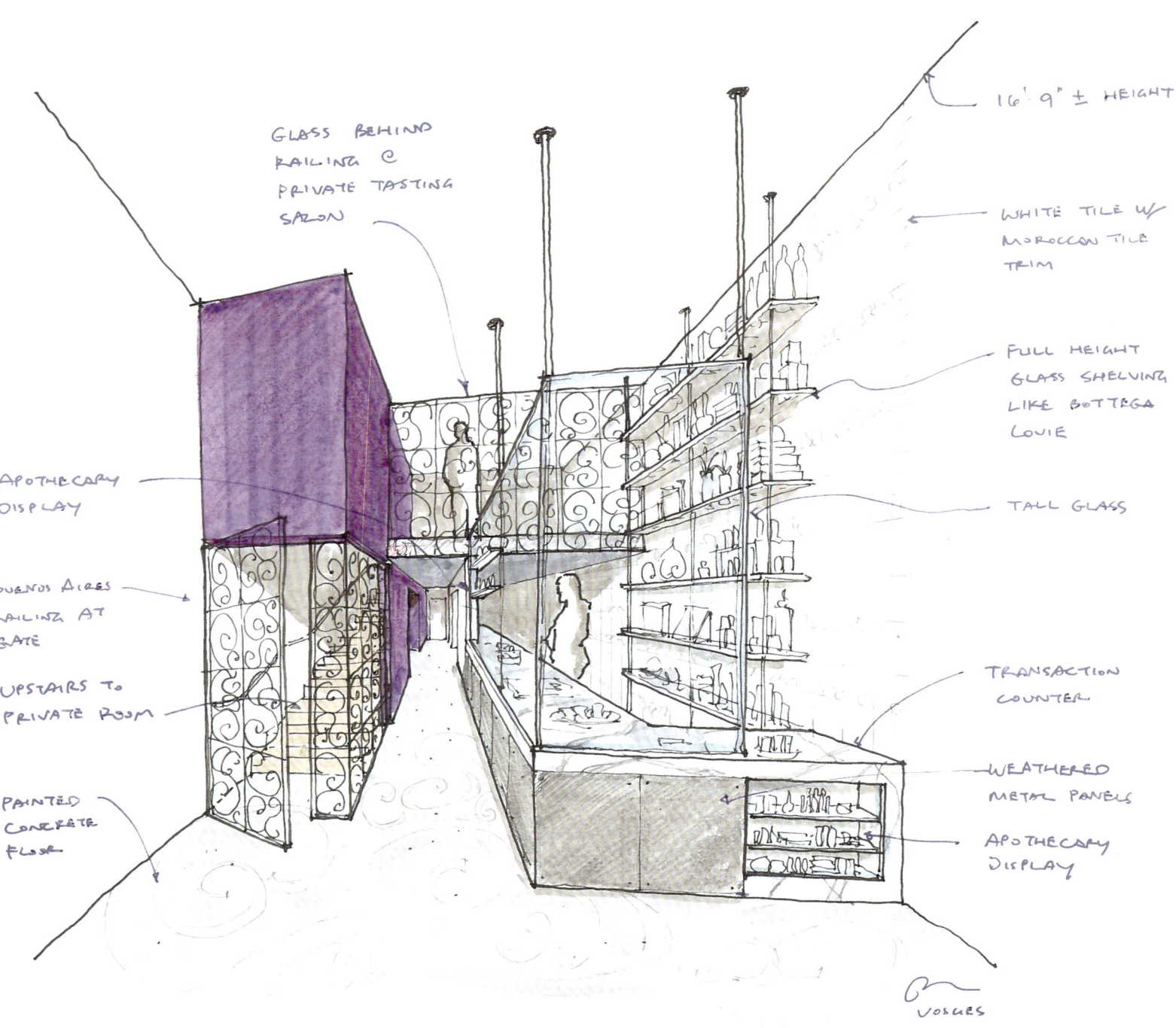

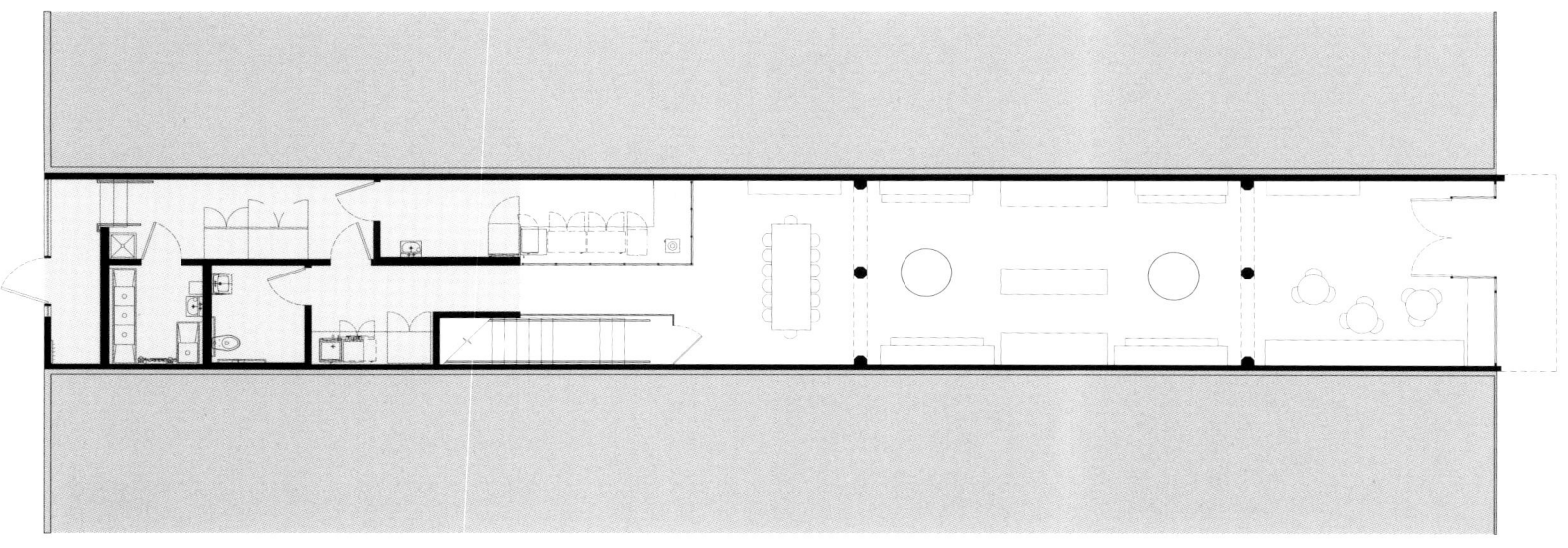

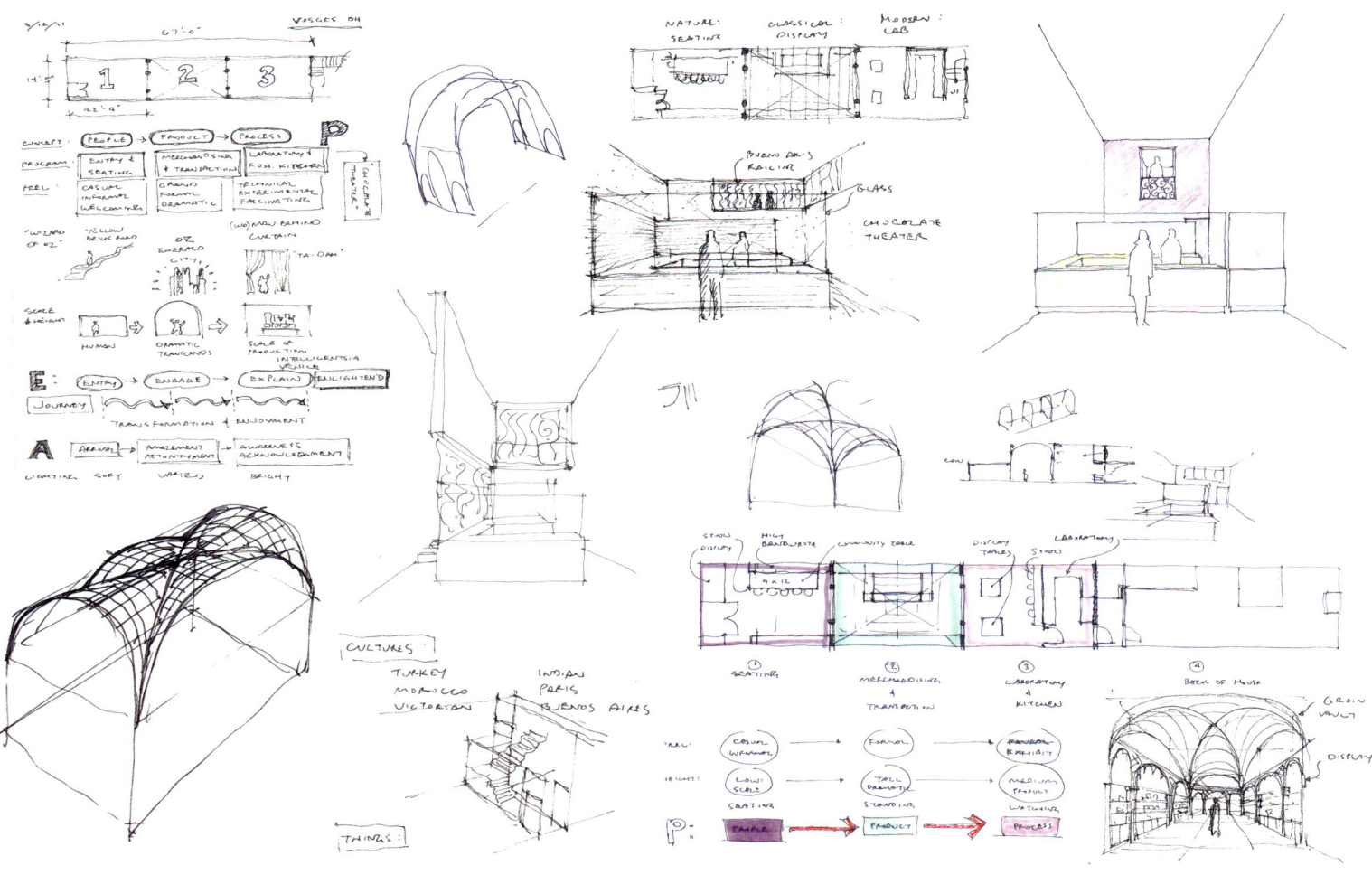

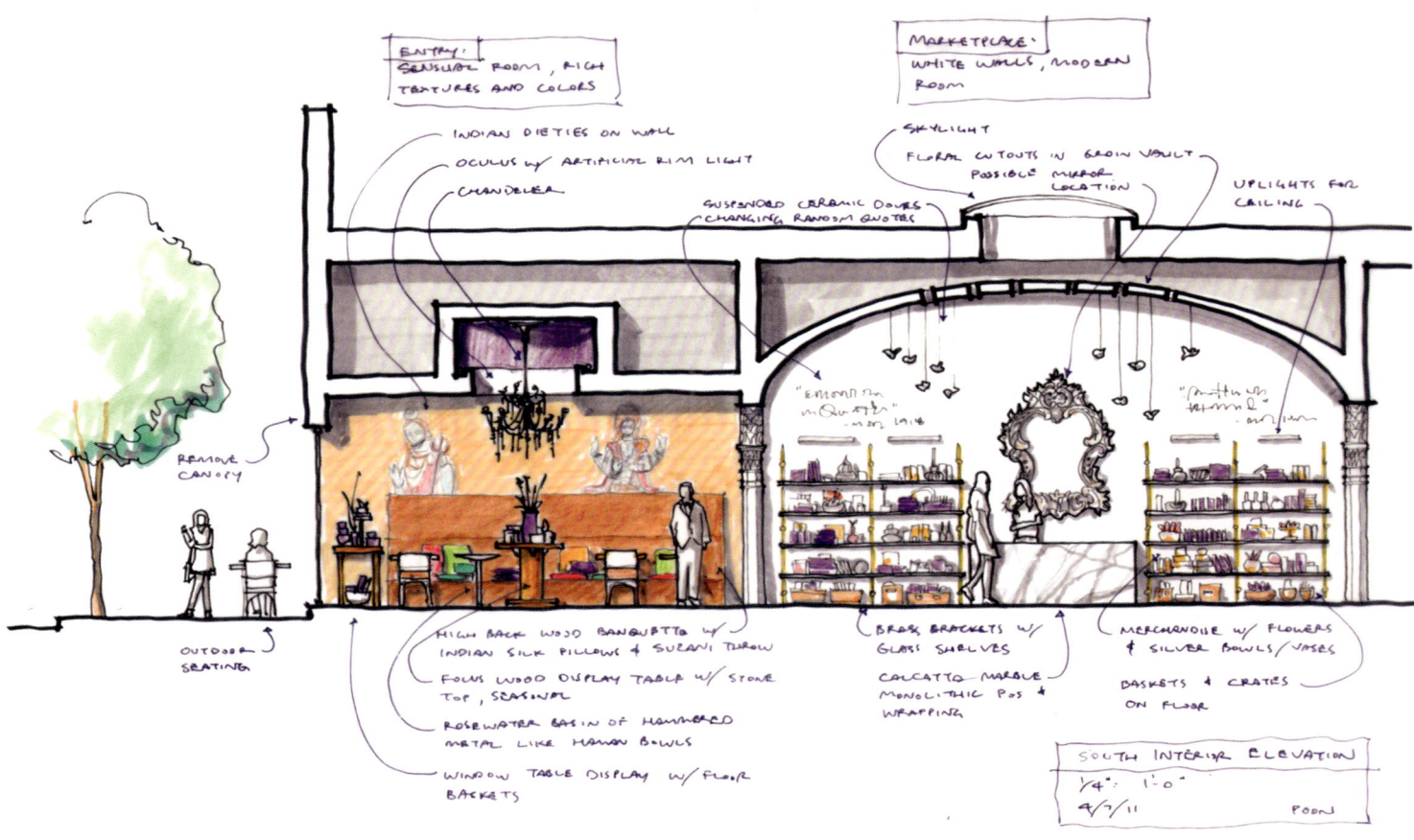

SELECT CHRONOLOGY
1996–2019

HERMOSA BEACH PIER AND MASTER PLAN
CALIFORNIA

MARTIN LUTHER KING MEMORIAL
WASHINGTON, D.C.

The redesign of a community space, waterfront, and pier offers the city a blank canvas. Suggested by the tilts, slopes, tears, and tucks of the plaza, a place of gathering is offered, where the city, sun, beach, ocean, and horizon can connect as one ensemble. Competition winner, Phase 1 completed in 1996.

Three thematic outdoor rooms—symbolizing the Man, the Movement, and the Message—connected by a meditative gravel path. The rooms are of various materials and experiences: concrete for courage, steel for strength, and glass for the future. 2001 competition entry.

WRAPPING PLANE HOUSE
LOS ANGELES, CALIFORNIA

The upper level of loft living, dining, and kitchen is framed in a continuously wrapping floor/wall/roof of wood planks. Private quarters are located on a lower level of this 2,700-square-foot Hollywood Hills residence. Unrealized, 2002.

HOLOCAUST HUMAN RIGHTS CENTER
UNIVERSITY OF MAINE, AUGUSTA

A 6,000-square-foot library addition hovers over the slope toward the future and the views, expressing poise and progress. The education resource center includes an exhibit hall, performance area, technology center, and classrooms. 2004 competition entry.

FLOATING ADDITION
WEST HOLLYWOOD, CALIFORNIA

A steel and glass 1,100-square-foot bedrooms addition floats over the existing 1,700-square-foot 1957 residence, with substantial air space in between for visual drama. The new floor is connected to the existing home through a minimal glass stair. Unrealized, 2004.

ROBBINS ELEMENTARY SCHOOL, ADDITIONS AND RENOVATION, TRENTON PUBLIC SCHOOLS
TRENTON, NEW JERSEY

Glass-clad classrooms engage the historic brick building, adding 99,500 square feet to the elementary school program. Old and new meet in the Instructional Atrium, a multi-story open space at the heart of the school. 2005 competition entry.

SANTA MONICA POWER YOGA
CALIFORNIA

Exercise studios, meditation rooms, retail, offices, and community functions comprise the 3,500-square-foot yoga center. A raw, richly colored, industrial character in contrast to the white-washed walls and bleached floors of other yoga studios. Completed 2005.

PERTH AMBOY HIGH SCHOOL
NEW JERSEY

The 900-student, 471,000-square-foot high school is scaled down into five academies and support functions, each with a distinct architectural character. The large canopy over the central spine unifies the school, expressing a dialogue between the individual and the community. 2005 competition entry. (Architecture for Education.)

WEST HIGH SCHOOL RENOVATION AND ADDITIONS
SCHOOL DISTRICT 129, AURORA, ILLINOIS

JOSS CUISINE
BEVERLY HILLS, CALIFORNIA

Additions to a 3,200-student, 419,000-square-foot high school include a math and science wing, horticulture lab and greenhouse, choral music wing and the three-court gymnasium. Completed 2005. (Architecture for Education, with associate architect, Gilfillan & Callahan Architects.)

The design for the 1,600-square-foot Chinese restaurant juxtaposes modern minimal expression with traditional Asian themes. A second-story private dining room is inserted over the kitchen, without altering the building exterior. Completed 2008.

CONTRABAND AND FREEDMEN'S MEMORIAL
ALEXANDRIA, VIRGINIA

An elevated wood and steel path hovers over the grave markers of slaves that have only recently been discovered. The journey passes through a grove of maples arriving at a gentle grass mound, the center of a new community park. 2008 competition entry, Honorable Mention.

MEMPHIS CAFÉ
MANHATTAN BEACH, CALIFORNIA

Internally LED-lit resin walls define the 110-seat restaurant. Through various glowing colors, the walls alter the character of the 3,200-square-foot place from day to night, from season to season. The exterior is covered with faux grass in an unexpected vertical application. Completed 2009.

PACIFICA CHRISTIAN HIGH SCHOOL
CULVER CITY, CALIFORNIA

Separate classroom wings focus on art, science/math, and history—with each wing defining an outdoor learning environment. Designed around a central garden, three amphitheaters take students up to the living roofs atop the classrooms. Accent buildings house the theater, library, and cafeteria. Unrealized, 2009.

MEDITATION RETREAT HOUSE
NATURAL BRIDGE, VIRGINIA

As the first of five projects for the Bodhi Path Buddhist Center, this modest meditation cabin was inspired by the region's vernacular architecture. The large interior space is adaptable through several 10-foot-tall sliding doors made from reclaimed barn lumber. Completed 2010.

AIR FORCE VILLAGE CHAPEL
SAN ANTONIO, TEXAS

S/B HOUSE
ENCINO, CALIFORNIA

For this retirement community, the triangular shape of the church references the Trinity and provides focus and direction—from the nave to the chancel, from the ground to the sky. Emblematic of the Air Force, the design expresses majesty, heroism, and strength. 2010 competition entry.

The 3,300-square-foot renovation and the 500-square-foot addition to a classic mid-century home explores the clients' interests in Japanese simplicity and 1930s Scandinavian design. Modern materials and details match the client's desire for an "Asian-Euro-Zen" aesthetic. Completed 2010.

SUSHI NOGUCHI
YORBA LINDA, CALIFORNIA

A simple idea transforms this 72-seat, 2,000-square-foot restaurant: the singular use of hickory wood slats. The wood details provide a continuous screen of privacy minimizing exterior heat and glare—folding up as the ceiling and folding down as wall paneling and built-in seating. Completed 2011.

IRVINE SPECTRUM CANOPIES
CALIFORNIA

Inspired by the children's game of Pick-Up Sticks, shade sculptures define a family-friendly park with fountain, amphitheater, maze, and playground—doubling as an urban sculpture. In progress.

VOSGES HAUT-CHOCOLAT CHOCOLATE FACTORY

CHICAGO, ILLINOIS

A 42,000-square-foot warehouse on the banks of the Chicago River is transformed into a chocolate factory. In addition to the production facility, the project includes the corporate headquarters, museum, retail, and restaurant, as well as a community park and river dock. Phase 1 completed 2012.

ALGORITHMIC TRELLIS

PASADENA, CALIFORNIA

For backyard shade structure, a parametric algorithm was developed to create a modulating field of small circular holes. The homeowner's interest in cooking is reflected in the translucent panels of polyethylene, the material used in kitchen cutting boards. Completed 2013.

RIVER OF LIFE CHRISTIAN CHURCH
SAN JOSE, CALIFORNIA

A renovation and addition to an existing 140,000-square-foot manufacturing facility transforms the building into a regional church and community center. The wood-clad 2,000-seat sanctuary resembles an ark sitting within a massive glass jewel box. Unrealized, 2013.

THE POINT LIFESTYLE CENTER
IRVINE, CALIFORNIA

A 120,000-square-foot Asian center featuring a supermarket, a Korean spa, a Japanese karaoke bar and a Chinese garden restaurant on four different levels. Escalators wrap the perimeter of the building, and a halo of trees restore the greenery displaced by the building's footprint. Unrealized, 2014.

HERITAGE FINE WINES
BEVERLY HILLS, CALIFORNIA

The showroom is an elliptical display of wine bottles with a sculpted, slatted ceiling that recalls the owner's love of clouds taken from memories of Paris. Other features include an artist's mural, zinc countertop, and antique European furniture. Completed 2014.

BUDDHIST DINING COMMONS
NATURAL BRIDGE, VIRGINIA

This community building provides 3,200 total square feet for the Bodhi Path Buddhist Center, including a dining hall, community lounge, visitor reception, retail area, and offices. The building gently bends in the middle, greeting visitors with a symbolic embrace. In progress.

C.A.P. MIXED-USE PROJECT
LOS ANGELES, CALIFORNIA

SPECTRUM PARKING
IRVINE, CALIFORNIA

The 10,000-square-foot, mixed-use project expresses the stacking of the three functions: retail and parking in board-formed concrete, offices in glass and aluminum, and five loft apartments clad in cedar panels and battens. In progress.

Water-jet-cut steel panels clad the existing 1,000-foot-long façade of a massive parking garage. Like soft fabric rippling in the wind, the pattern in the steel captures the visual quality of a translucent wedding veil. In progress.

OMBRA WINE BAR
THE AMERICANA AT BRAND, GLENDALE, CALIFORNIA

Ombra Wine Bar consists of an outdoor bar, garden, and event space shaded by a garden of trees fabricated from translucent resin panels. In progress.

BUDDHIST TEMPLE
NATURAL BRIDGE, VIRGINIA

Poon Design's third completed project for the Bodhi Path Buddhist Center, this simple form provides a backdrop for a bronze Buddha statue from Asia. Hand crafted by community labor employing authentic heavy timber construction. Completed 2016.

SANTA CLARA SQUARE
CALIFORNIA

In a mixed-use development of several city blocks, a dozen light installations deliver artistic experiences. Unrealized, 2016.

THE CONTAINER YARD
LOS ANGELES, CALIFORNIA

Four existing warehouses and two large open spaces are transformed into a 40,000-square-foot arts park and social/cultural center on a 1.4-acre site. The architectural interventions are variations on a single theme: prefabricated steel shipping containers. Unrealized, 2017.

14TH SHAMARPA RELIQUARY BUILDING
NATURAL BRIDGE, VIRGINIA

DOHENY PLAZA
WEST HOLLYWOOD, CALIFORNIA

This sacred structure preserves the relics of Shamar Rinpoche, the distinguished Red Hat Lama of Tibet, within a gold-leafed stupa. Poon Design's fourth completed building for the Bodhi Path Buddhist Center explores a crafted architecture of both human and spiritual hands. Completed 2018.

A 13-story condominium tower is re-imagined in form and pattern. The renovated 102,000-square-foot high-rise will have a new entry addition highlighted by a 100-foot-long entry canopy of stainless steel and backlit translucent acrylic. Under construction.

COLBY RESIDENCE
LOS ANGELES, CALIFORNIA

Atop a renovated one-story house sits the new, wood, second-story addition. The four-bedroom, 2,900-square-foot residence displays wood siding in various widths installed horizontally and vertically. Under construction.

MALIBU GOLF CLUB AND RESORT
MALIBU, CALIFORNIA

This project is for a community of 11 5,000-square-foot hotel villas in a 640-acre golf resort. Each villa comprises four bedrooms and a shared common area. Open air and pinwheel in configuration, the rooms frame views while assuring privacy. In progress.

LINEA: MODERN COURTYARD
PALM SPRINGS, CALIFORNIA

ENTRY WALL, THE RITZ-CARLTON AND JW MARRIOTT
LOS ANGELES, CALIFORNIA

The 5,400-square-foot, three-bedroom production house completes the architect's design of a 14-home gated community. Capturing the luxury and glamour of the California desert lifestyle, this courtyard concept arranges the residence and guest house around a 36-foot-diameter swimming pool. Completed 2019.

At the porte cochere and main entrance to the 54-level luxury hotel and residential highrise, this sculptural wall blends architecture with art. 260 shaped steel fins at 10'-6" tall comprises a 87-foot long sculptural statement of contour and texture. Under construction.

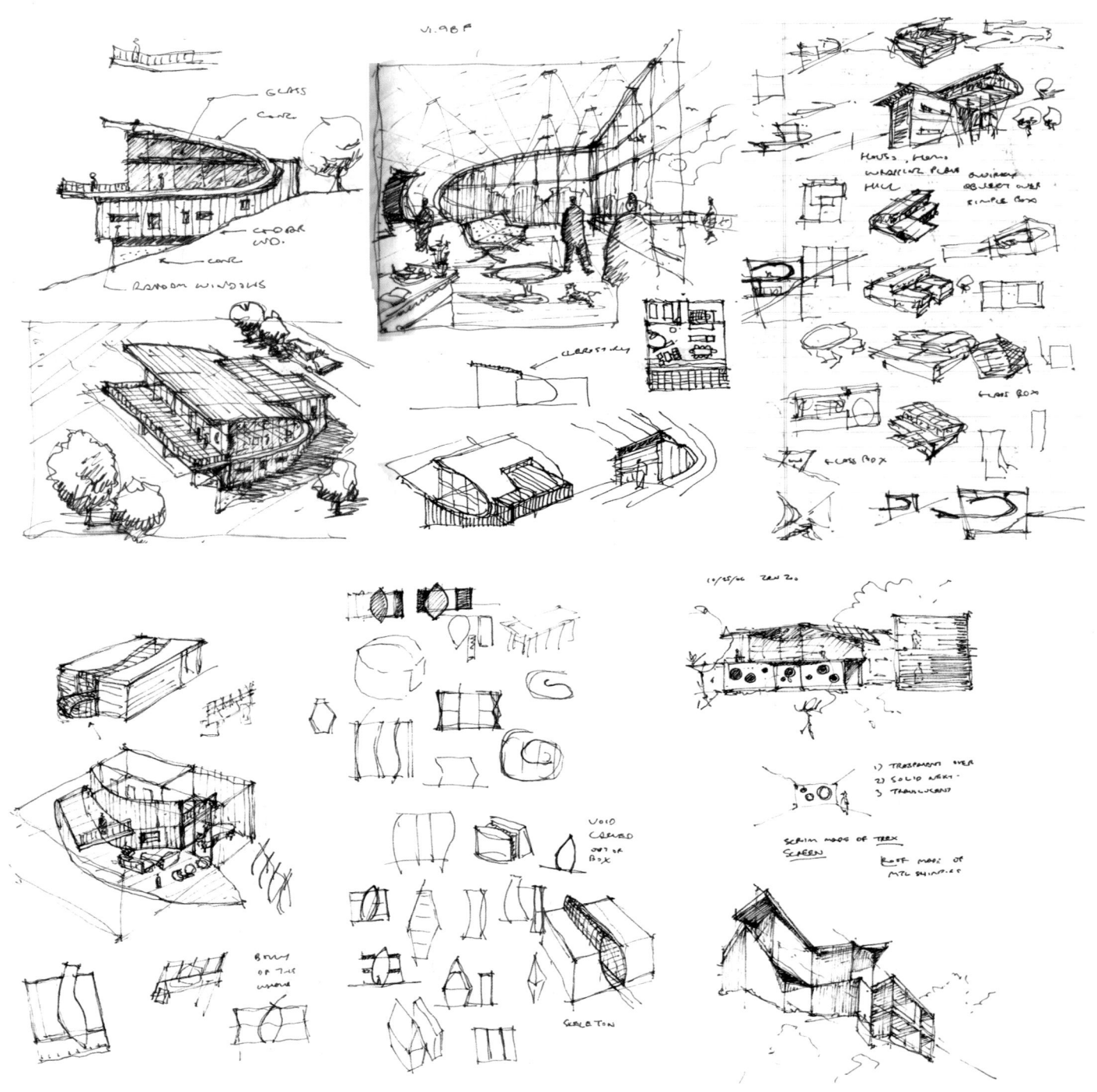

FIRM PROFILE

Poon Design Inc., a multi-disciplinary practice, offers services in architecture and interiors, programming and master planning, furniture design and graphics, and other design-related services. Launched in 2001, the company's award-winning design talents serve national and international clients, with over 300 completed projects of various types: residential, commercial, educational, religious, cultural, and mixed-use. The work of Poon Design has received over 50 national honors, and has been featured in the *Wall Street Journal*, the *Los Angeles Times*, *Dwell*, *Los Angeles Magazine*, *Architectural Record*, *Architecture*, and *Interior Design*.

Poon Design received the 2018 National Design Award for Best in Housing, from the American Institute of Architects. The studio is also recognized for the re-envisioning of America's tract-housing industry, with two-dozen national design awards from the AIA, NAHB, and BIA.

Anthony Poon has worked on over 50 education projects ranging from PreK–12 to universities. Anthony was awarded the National Grand Prize from Learning by Design in 2005 and 2006, the highest honor given for educational projects in the country.

Poon Design has completed over 40 restaurants, and was awarded the 2009 and 2011 International Design Award for Best Restaurant Design from the American Institute of Architects.

Alongside Poon Design's commercial projects for some of the country's most prominent developers, the studio also serves non-profit clients, such as master planning and several ongoing projects for an international Buddhist foundation and campus.

ANTHONY POON AIA, LEED GA

Educated as a multi-disciplinary designer, Anthony Poon is an award-winning architect and musician. Spanning three decades of professional experience, he is a LEED-accredited architect licensed in California and Virginia, and a member of the American Institute of Architects—as well as a classical pianist, mixed-media artist, and published author. Poon received his Masters in Architecture from Harvard University and his Bachelor of Arts from the University of California, Berkeley, magna cum laude.

He is a frequent public speaker at national and regional conferences and panels, as well as schools and universities. Poon is also a member of the Modern and Contemporary Art Council for the Los Angeles County Museum of Art.

Poon was a performing artist for the 2012 Architects in Concert, and a selected mixed-media artist for national art shows, www.anthonypoonart.com. Poon's book, *Sticks and Stones / Steel and Glass: One Architect's Journey*, has received critical acclaim, and he writes regularly on architecture and design at www.anthonypoon.com.

SELECT AWARDS FOR POON DESIGN INC.

National Design Award,
Best in Housing Design
The American Institute of Architects
Linea Residence G, Palm Springs,
California, 2018

Most Innovative Residential Design,
Linea Residence G
The 2018 Innovators in Design, Build
Review

Most Outstanding Residential Design
Services, California
The 2018 Innovators in Design, Build
Review

Grand Prize,
Best Single Family Detached Home,
Gold Nugget Awards
Pacific Coast Builders Conference
Horizon Residence, Alta Verde Escena,
Palm Springs, California, 2016

Excellence Award,
Education Facility and Restaurant
Architecture, Build Architecture
Awards
Staffordshire, England, 2016

Award of Merit,
Best Single Family Detached Home,
Gold Nugget Awards
Pacific Coast Builders Conference
Horizon Residence, Alta Verde Escena,
Palm Springs, California, 2016

Award of Merit,
Best Single Family Detached Home,
Gold Nugget Awards
Pacific Coast Builders Conference
Residence Z-3, Alta Verde Coral
Mountain, La Quinta, California, 2014

Award of Merit,
Best Single Family Detached Home,
Gold Nugget Awards
Pacific Coast Builders Conference
Residence Modern Villa, Alta Verde
Monte Sereno, Palm Springs,
California, 2014

National Innovation Award,
Best For-Sale Community, Best of 50+
National Association of Home Builders
Alta Verde Coral Mountain, La Quinta,
California, 2014

National Gold Award,
Best Detached Home, Best of 50+
National Association of Home Builders
Modern Villa, Alta Verde Monte Sereno,
Palm Springs, California, 2014

National Gold Award,
Best For-Sale Community, Best of 50+
National Association of Home Builders
Alta Verde Coral Mountain, La Quinta,
California, 2014

National Silver Award,
Best Single Family Home
National Association of Home Builders
Residence B-3, Alta Verde Escena, Palm
Springs, California, 2014

National Silver Award,
Best Detached Community
National Association of Home Builders
Alta Verde Coral Mountain, La Quinta,
California, 2014

Award Winner,
Industrial Redevelopment of the Year,
Awards of Excellence
National Association of Industrial
and Office Parks
Vosges Haut Chocolat Factory, Chicago,
Illinois, 2013

National Platinum Award,
Detached Home Built for Sale,
Best in American Living
National Association of Home Builders
Residence J-3, Alta Verde Coral
Mountain, La Quinta, California, 2013

Best in Region, Pacific,
Best in American Living
National Association of Home Builders
Residence J-3, Alta Verde Coral
Mountain, La Quinta, California, 2013

National Gold Award,
Detached Home Built for Sale,
Best in American Living
National Association of Home Builders
Residence B-3, Alta Verde Escena, Palm
Springs, California, 2013

Award of Merit,
Best Single Family Detached Home,
Gold Nugget Awards
Pacific Coast Builders Conference
Residence L-3, Alta Verde Escena, Palm
Springs, California, 2013

International Design Award for Best
Restaurant, People's Choice
The American Institute of Architects,
Los Angeles Chapter
Mendocino Farms, Marina Del Rey,
California, 2011

International Design Award for Best
Restaurant
The American Institute of Architects,
Los Angeles Chapter
Chaya Downtown, Los Angeles,
California, 2009

Merit Award
The American Institute of Architects,
Cabrillo Chapter
Hermosa Beach Pier, California, 1995

SELECT AWARDS FOR ANTHONY POON WITH ARCHITECTURE FOR EDUCATION

Outstanding Design Award
American School and University Magazine
Institute for Collaboration in Education, Aurora, Illinois, 2008

Grand Prize
NSBA National Exhibition of School Architecture
Herget Middle School, Aurora, Illinois, 2007

Citation of Excellence
Learning By Design
Herget Middle School, Aurora, Illinois, 2007

Award of Distinction for "Excellence in the Design of Educational Environments"
Illinois Association of School Boards
Herget Middle School, Aurora, Illinois, 2007

2006 Educational Environments
The Joint Annual Conference of IASB, IASA, and IASBO
Herget Middle School, Aurora, Illinois, 2007

Honorable Mention,
Education Design Showcase
School Planning & Management
Herget Middle School, Aurora, Illinois, 2007

Design Award
Impact on Learning
Herget Middle School, Aurora, Illinois, 2007

Citation Award
The American Institute of Architects CAE, Educational Facilities Design
Feather River Academy, Yuba City, California, 2007

Award of Distinction for Excellence
Joint Annual Conference of IASB, IASA, and IASBO, Chicago
Greenman Elementary School, Aurora, Illinois, 2006

Honor Award
DesignShare, School Construction News, Edutopia, and Schools for Life
Feather River Academy, Yuba City, California, 2006

Merit Award, DesignShare
School Construction News, Edutopia, and Schools for Life
Herget Middle School, Aurora, Illinois, 2006

Grand Prize
NSBA National Exhibition of School Architecture
Greenman Elementary School, Aurora, Illinois, 2006

Honorable Mention, Outstanding Architecture and Design in Education
School Planning & Management
Greenman Elementary School, Aurora, Illinois, 2006

2006 Educational Environments
The Joint Annual Conference of IASB, IASA, and IASBO
Greenman Elementary School, Aurora, Illinois, 2006

Merit Award
The American Institute of Architects, Inland California Chapter
Greenman Elementary School, Aurora, Illinois, 2005

Citation Award
The American Institute of Architects CAE, Educational Facilities Design
Feather River Academy, Yuba City, California, 2007

2005 Honor Society, KnowledgeWorks Foundation
Greenman Elementary School, Aurora, Illinois, 2005

Merit Award
DesignShare and School Construction News
Greenman Elementary School, Aurora, Illinois, 2005

Impact on Learning Award
School & College Planning & Management
Greenman Elementary School, Aurora, Illinois, 2005

Grand Prize
Learning by Design National Highest Honor
Greenman Elementary School, Aurora, Illinois, 2005

Design Citation, Architectural Portfolio
American School & University Magazine
Greenman Elementary School, Aurora, Illinois, 2004

PUBLICATIONS ON THE WORK

Webb, Michael, "Anthony Poon Delivers Modernism to Tract Housing," *Form* magazine January/February 2019

Wang, Lucy, "Award-winning Palm Springs home embraces the California climate in sustainable style," *inhabitat.com*, July 11, 2018

Garfield, Leanna, "The most exceptional new homes in North America, according to architects," *BusinessInsider.com*, May 20, 2018

Johnson, Sara, "AIA Announces the 11 Winners of the 2018 Housing Awards," *architectmagazine.com*, May 18, 2018

Lee, Euno, "This New Pasadena Korean Barbeque Restaurant Takes the Genre to New Heights," *Eater Los Angeles*, September 12, 2017

Flemming, Jack, "First of 14 minimalist-modern homes hits the market in Palm Springs," *Los Angeles Times*, August 24, 2017

Lawetzki, Michelle, "Anthony Poon: In Tune With The Process," *LA Home*, Winter–Spring 2016

McLaughlin, Katy, "The Ranch House, Reinvented," the *Wall Street Journal*, July 12, 2015

Stamp, Elizabeth, "The Ten Most Beautiful Candy Shops," *Architectural Digest*, February 1, 2015

"Alta Verde Group Sweeps Top Design Awards at National Convention," *Nasdaq OMX / Globe Newswire*, February 21, 2014

Bingham, Lisa, "The Dumpling Connection," *FormMag.net*, January 9, 2014

Nakano, Craig, "Modern for the Masses: Escena Palm Springs, SoCal's First Modern Tract Houses in Decades," *Los Angeles Times*, July 26, 2013

Lubell, Sam, "Poon Design brings handcrafted charm to Mendocino Farms' newest outpost in Los Angeles," the *Architect's Newspaper, ArchPaper.com*, February 19, 2013

Alif, Veronica, "Poon Design Uses Parametric Algorithms to Create Geometric Trellis in Pasadena," the *Architect's Newspaper, ArchPaper.com*, November 13, 2012

McDonald, Kathy A., "Desert Modernism Blooms in Palm Springs," *Los Angeles Confidential, LA-Confidential-Magazine.com*, November 2012

Coleman, Laura, "Three New Luxury Developments In The Desert To Tempt Westside Buyers," *Beverly Hills Courier*, August 17, 2012

"The 8th Annual Restaurant Design Awards," *Dwell*, June 2012

Nakano, Craig, "2012 Restaurant Design Award Finalists Announced," *latimes.com*, May 24, 2012

Galarza, Daniela, "Mendocino Farms to Open at Third & Fairfax on May 22," *eater.com*, April 30, 2012

Abramian-Mott, Alexandria, "Sweet Deals," *Angeleno Interiors*, Spring 2012

"Alta Verde Escena. A New View on Modernism," *San Francisco Chronicle*, February 2012

"Alta Verde Introduces 'This Century Modern' to Palm Springs," the *Wall Street Journal*, February 24, 2012

Meinhold, Bridgette, "Bel Air Presbyterian Preschool is an Eco Village for Learning," *inhabitat.com*, August 15, 2011

"Manhattan Beach Mixed Use Project Boasts Green Room Big Enough For Lawn Sports," *inhabitat.com*, August 8, 2011

Kraege, Lisa, "Modern for the Masses," *Form*, July/August 2011

"Architects group gives restaurant, lounge design awards," *Los Angeles Times*, June 24, 2011

Tracy, Laura Williams, "Poon Design. Mixing Mediums and Artistic Talents for Unique Results," *American Builders Quarterly*, March/April 2011

Boone, Lisa, "Pro Portfolio: Midcentury Update in Encino," *Los Angeles Times*, January 17, 2011

"New Mendocino Farms Debuts Monday," *LosAngelesDowntownNews.com*, November 11, 2009

Atwal, Heidi, "Design, Redefined. Chaya Downtown Marries Whimsy with Age-Old Tradition," *SOMA*, August 2009, Volume 23.5

"2009 Restaurant Design Awards," *Form*, September/October 2009

Nakano, Craig, "The Good of Small Things," *Los Angeles Times*, June 6, 2009

Virbila, S. Irene, "The Review: Chaya Downtown," *Los Angeles Times*, May 20, 2009

Brown, Danny, "Builder sees future in green roofs," *Easy Reader*, November 29, 2007

Harris, Katy, "The Dish: Health. The Big Stretch," *Angeleno*, July 2005

"2005 Grand Prize Winners, Excellence in School Design," *Learning By Design*, Issue 14, 2005

Hanley, Matt, "Greenman School is mixture of light, arts," the *Beacon News*, September 1, 2003

Moore, Mary Ellen, "New West school to keep close to rural roots," the *Beacon News*, May 20, 2003

PRESENTATIONS, PANELS, AND PODCASTS

"Architecture & Music: High Concept Takes Center Stage," Wende Museum, Culver City, May 22, 2019

"Design Influencer Roundtable, Convo by Design," Pacific Design Center, West Hollywood, April 18, 2019

"The Business of Art and Interiors: Leveraging Smart Investments with the Intangible," *WestWeek*, Pacific Design Center, West Hollywood, March 20, 2019

Interview on *Mottek on Money*, with Frank Mottek, KNX 10.70 Newsradio, Los Angeles, California, February 16, 2019

"Celluloid Heroes," *Modernism Week*, Palm Springs, California, February 15, 2019

"Architecture and Music: The Imperfection of Perfection," Idyllwild Arts Academy, California, February 8, 2019

"Architect – Anthony Poon: The Art Within Music and Architecture," *Convo by Design*, November 1, 2018

"Silicon Beach Design: The Hub of Design Innovation," *westedge/:form*, October 20, 2018

"Anthony Poon," *Focus TV and LA/Home*, August 10, 2018

"Sticks & Stones, Steel & Glass: One Architect's Journey," *Modernism Week*, Palm Springs, California, February 23, 2018

"Architecture and Music: The Imperfection of Perfection," *This Modern Life: A Design Field Day*, Helms Bakery, Los Angeles, California, June 10, 2017

Architects in Concert, Santa Monica, California, October 2012

Guest professor, University of Southern California, School of Architecture, Fall 2004

PHOTOGRAPHY AND IMAGE CREDITS

Al Forster: 201 (left)

Anthony Poon: 5, 7, 8, 11, 20, 21, 44, 58, 59, 60–61, 62 (top), 82, 84, 104–105, 106 (top), 114–115, 123 (top), 124–25, 134, 135, 137 (top), 144, 155, 156, 157, 161 (bottom), 163, 169, 170, 186, 190, 191, 193, 194, 195, 196, 199, 201 (right), 202 (left), 203 (left), 204 (right), 205 (left), 207, 212 (left), 219

Architecture for Education: 94, 123 (bottom)

Ballogg Photography: cover (image wrapping on spine), front end page facing title page and back end page facing acknowledgments, 28–29, 31, 34, 37, 38, 90, 92–93, 96, 97, 99 (bottom), 101, 117, 118–19, 120, 121, 126, 127, 215 (right), 216 (left)

Chris Miller: 16 (bottom two images), 17 (top left and bottom right), 55, 57, 63, 64 (bottom), 65

David Blank: cover (front right), 24, 26–27, 33, 36 (bottom), 218 (left)

Elon Schoenholz: 204 (left)

George Guttenberg: front end spread

Grant Bozigian: 12, 221

Gregg Segal: cover (back left), 81, 83, 85, 87, 141, 142, 143, 145, 147, 148, 149, 150, 151, 167, 168, 171, 172, 174, 175, 176, 178, 179, 180, 182, 183, 184–85, back end spread

Gregory Blore: 103, 106 (bottom), 107, 110, 111, 112, 113

Hunter Kerhart: 39, 41, 42–43, 45, 48, 49

James Butchart: 17 (bottom left) 47, 50, 51, 53

Lambros Photography Inc.: 95

Lance Gerber: 16 (top two images), 67, 68–69, 70 (bottom), 73, 74, 77, 78 (bottom), 79

Locke Pleninger, Alta Verde Group: 17 (top right), 71

Lukas Ruzbasan, Encore Design Studio: 212 (right), 216 (right), 217 (left)

Marrakesh Designs Ltd.: 198

Mike Amaya: 128, 131, 133, 137 (bottom), 202 (right), 203 (right), 208 (left), 211 (left), 217 (right)

Niloo Hosseini: 214 (left), 215 (left)

Olek Zemplinski, bioLINIA: 15, 206 (left)

Poon Design Inc.: 19, 30, 36 (top), 46, 56, 62 (bottom), 64 (top), 70 (top), 72, 78 (top), 86, 98, 99 (top), 109, 122, 136, 146, 152, 154, 158, 159, 160, 161 (top), 164, 165, 173, 181, 188–89, 192, 197, 205 (right), 208 (right), 209, 210, 211 (right), 213, 215 (right), 218 (right)

Sean Rosenthal: 206 (right)

ACKNOWLEDGMENTS

Thank you to Michael Webb for believing that a monograph on our work would be a worthwhile endeavor. I acknowledge my publishing team at ORO Editions—Gordon Goff, Jake Anderson, and Pablo Mandel—for bringing this book to life, and thank you to Christine Anderson of Communication Arts+Design for connecting the dots.

Akin to the performance of a jazz ensemble, architecture is created through a collaborative effort. Thank you to the ensemble at Poon Design Inc., where each new project is an adventure with an unknown but thrilling end. Thanks to Principal John Kim and the many contributors over the years: Bryan Bethem, Shani Cho, Esther Chung, Debra Hakimi, Carlos Hernandez, Niloo Hosseini, Artemisa Gjergo, Jim Gilette, Ben Kalenik, Cynthia Kraus, Sandy Lee, Barbara Leon, Jared Licano, Noreena Manio, Charles Proffitt, Seth Trotter, Anushri Vachhani, Robert Weimer, Khin Zaw, and many others. A special acknowledgment to Artemisa for meticulously creating the floor plans and site plans within this monograph.

Thank you also to the team at Architecture for Education: Co-Founder and Principal Gaylaird Christopher, along with Rachel Adams, Jack Avakyan, Michael Bulander, Miriam Grethel, Tony Hensley, Caroline Kerr, Satsuki Kitagawa, Dennis Roney, Nick Saelow, Sita Torres, and Yong Yoo.

Architecture does not exist without clients, engineers, consultants, and contractors. Collaborative partners, to name a few, include Mike Valles and Scott Allen of Interior Illusions, Nicole Cuneo-Williams of Prest Vuksic Architects, Cordogan, Clark & Associates, and Lazar Design/Build. Thanks to the design leadership of Andrew Adler and the construction prowess of Russell Jones, both of Alta Verde Group. Also, to Dr. Sherry Eagle for considering me a partner in her vision for the highest quality education of our children. Thank you to my long list of clients, colleagues, and team members.

I offer my personal gratitude to Christine Fang for believing in me since the early days of high school and even today. To David E. Martin who has mentored me—in addition to the value of good architecture, David has shown me what compassion and kindness can create. Lastly, without my two amazingly wonderful and curious daughters, Ella and Lily, my existence would be without grace, joy, and delight.